SKITS AND SPOOFS
FOR YOUNG ACTORS

D1713600

Skits and Spoofs
for
Young Actors

by VAL R. CHEATHAM

*One-act, royalty-free plays,
skits, and spoofs
for the amateur stage*

Publishers   PLAYS, INC.   *Boston*

Library of Congress Cataloging in Publication Data

Cheatham, Val R.
  Skits and spoofs for young actors.

  CONTENTS: Big, Bad Wolf at the door. — Jack, the beanstalk, and chicken. — The Tortoise and the Hare hit the road. — Meet Dr. Frankenstein. [etc.]
  1. Children's plays. [1. Plays] I. Title.
PN6120.S8C5   812'.5'4   77-23906
ISBN 0-8238-0220-5

Contents

SKITS AND SPOOFS
FOR YOUNG ACTORS

Big, Bad Wolf at the Door

Red Riding Hood gets an offer she can't refuse . . .

Characters
NARRATOR
RED RIDING HOOD
BIG BAD WOLF
THE FATHER-IN-LAW, *a mobster*
BIG AL⎫
JUNIOR⎭ *his henchmen*
GRANDMA

SCENE 1

BEFORE RISE: NARRATOR *enters and addresses audience.*

NARRATOR: The story you are about to see is true. Only the cast will be changed to protect it from the audience, the playwright, or anyone else who may disagree with our rendition. It is about Little Red Riding Hood, who has taken a basket of goodies and gone through the forest to visit her poor, old, sick Grandma. And let me tell you, if you think a person

3

has got problems on the streets today, watch what happens to innocent Little Red. (*Exits*)

SETTING: *The forest. This scene may be played before curtain.*

AT RISE: BIG BAD WOLF *is leaning against a tree, flipping a coin.* RED RIDING HOOD *enters, skipping, with a basket over her arm.*

RED (*Singsong*): Oh, I'm off to see my grandma — my wonderful, wonderful grandma ...

WOLF (*Breezy*): Hello, there, doll-face ... you going my way?

RED: I'm on my way through the forest to see —

WOLF (*Interrupting*): Don't tell me, sweets, let me guess. (*Looks her over*) A red hood ... a basket of goodies ... I'll bet you're Little Red Riding Hood, and you're on your way to visit your poor, old, sick Grandma — right?

RED: Yes! How did you know that? (*She puts her hand to mouth, startled.*) Oh my goodness! I'll bet you're the Big Bad Wolf!

WOLF: Oh, little lady (*Clutches heart lugubriously*) — your accusation pains me. I may be a wolf — and I may be big — but bad? (*Shakes head*) No! What's in the basket, kid?

RED (*Ignoring question*): If you're not bad, why does everybody say you are?

WOLF: Professional jealousy, what else? I'm big and hungry — I mean handsome. How can they help envying me? (*Eagerly*) What's in the basket, huh?

RED: It must be awful to have people saying all those

untrue things about you!

WOLF: You know it, girlie, you know it. Actually, if the truth were known, I spend ninety percent of my time looking for ways to help people. Here, that basket looks heavy. Let me help you carry it. (*Reaches for basket*)

RED: No! (*Pulls basket away*) It's not heavy at all.

WOLF: But I just want to help you. (*Smiles at audience*)

RED: Thank you, no. I need to do it myself so I can earn five points on a Girl Scout merit badge.

WOLF (*Angrily*): Look! I'm going to help you whether you like it or not! (*Grabs basket and starts to exit, just as* FATHER-IN-LAW, BIG AL *and* JUNIOR *enter.* WOLF *quickly turns, and returns basket to* RED.) Uh-oh! I just remembered that I promised my mother's carpentry class to come by today and tell them how the Three Little Pigs built their homes. So long! (*Exits hurriedly at opposite side of stage*)

RED (*To audience*): Isn't that a friendly gesture! Why would anyone call him bad?

FATHER-IN-LAW (*To* RED): Hey, you with the basket! Come here. (RED *turns, looks at* FATHER-IN-LAW, *and points to herself.*)

RED: Me?

FATHER-IN-LAW: Yeah! You with the red bandanna. Do yourself a favor and come here to the Father-in-Law. (*Points to himself*)

BIG AL (*Putting backs of wrists to belt*): Come on, come on! The Father-in-Law doesn't like to be kept waiting.

JUNIOR: Look at that outfit, Father-in-Law. She's dressed up like Little Red Riding Hood on her way to take some goodies to her grandma's house. (*Laughs*)

RED (*Innocently*): You're right. I am Little Red Riding Hood and I'm on my way to my poor, sick grandma's. How did you know?

JUNIOR (*Raising arm menacingly*): Why, you little punk! I —

RED (*Stepping forward and pointing finger at* JUNIOR): Touch me and I'll tell my grandma on you!

BIG AL: Let me take care of her, Father-in-Law. (FATHER-IN-LAW *snaps fingers and motions both* JUNIOR *and* BIG AL *to step back.*)

FATHER-IN-LAW: Hey, Red, I like your spunk! Don't mind my boys, here. (*Pointing*) That one is Junior, and this is Big Al.

RED: *Big* Al? He doesn't look very big to me!

FATHER-IN-LAW (*Looking at* AL): That's because he's not completely dressed. He looks much bigger when he's wearing his machine gun. Get it? (*Looks at* AL *and* JUNIOR *and begins to chuckle. They immediately begin to laugh. When all three are laughing loudly* FATHER-IN-LAW *stops laughing and snaps his fingers.* AL *and* JUNIOR *quickly stop also.*)

RED: I don't know what's so funny. I *am* Little Red Riding Hood and I'm on my way to take this basket of goodies to my poor, sick grandma.

FATHER-IN-LAW: Sure, kid, sure. Tell me — what was that Wolf doing with your basket, huh?

RED: He was trying to help me. You might say he was

doing me a favor.

FATHER-IN-LAW: Look, any favors done around here, I do them, understand? You want a favor, you come to me — the Father-in-Law.

RED: But, I don't want a favor. I just want to take this basket of goodies to my poor, sick grandma.

FATHER-IN-LAW: Oh, yeah? That must be an important basket. So you do *me* a favor and tell me what's in it. (*Motions to* AL *and* JUNIOR, *who start toward* RED.)

RED: It's only goodies for my grandma, I tell you! (*She starts to step back, but* BIG AL *steps behind her and* JUNIOR *steps in front of her.*)

JUNIOR (*Taking basket*): Sure, sure! (*Hands basket to* FATHER-IN-LAW)

FATHER-IN-LAW (*Holding basket with one hand, testing its weight*): Say, now, that's heavy! Tell me, Red, do you make your goodies with bricks? (*Laughs.* JUNIOR *and* AL *laugh, too. He cuts them off with a snap of his fingers.*) I'm just going to have to reach into this basket and find out for myself.

RED: Oh, no, you don't. (*Seizes basket*) I'm taking these goodies to my poor, sick grandma. (*Runs off and exits*)

FATHER-IN-LAW: Hey, Red, come back here! (FATHER-IN-LAW *looks at* JUNIOR *and* AL.) She didn't give me a chance to make her an offer she couldn't refuse! (*Quick curtain*)

*   *   *   *   *

SCENE 2

BEFORE RISE: NARRATOR *enters and speaks to audience.*

NARRATOR: Scene 2 of our tension-filled drama takes place in Grandma's house. But before we begin, let's recap the highlights of Scene 1. Little Red Riding Hood started to Grandma's house with a basket of goodies — a normal circumstance; then, there was danger as the Wolf tried to take the goodies for himself; and finally, there was intrigue, as the Wolf was foiled by the entrance of the Father-in-Law, who is interested only in doing favors. Now we'll do everybody a favor and begin Scene 2. (*Exits.*)

SETTING: *Grandma's living room. There is an easy chair center. Beside it is a table with long cloth reaching to floor.*

AT RISE: GRANDMA *is sitting in easy chair with thermometer in her mouth, ice bag on her head, and blanket tucked around her legs and feet. She removes thermometer, looks at it, and puts it on table.*

GRANDMA (*Groaning*): Oh, my! I just have to stop this living it up and dancing till all hours of the night. Comes a time when a body is just too old. (*There is a knock on door.*) Good grief — not company! I can tell already this is just not going to be my day. (*Calls*) Come in! (WOLF *enters.*)

WOLF: Surprise, Granny! It's me!

GRANDMA (*Disgusted*): I knew it! I knew it! The day started badly and already it's taken a turn for the worse!

WOLF: Guess what, Granny? Little Red is on her way here now with a basket of goodies — and I mean to get them. (*He smacks lips and rubs stomach, then takes a large handkerchief from pocket.*)

GRANDMA: Ten thousand children's stories in the world and I have to be in this one! (WOLF *ties handkerchief over* GRANDMA*'s mouth.*)

WOLF: There you are, Granny. Keep a stiff upper lip! (GRANDMA *mumbles angrily. There is a knock at door.*)

RED (*From offstage*): Yoo-hoo! It's me! Little Red Riding Hood!

WOLF: Wow! If Little Red gets any faster, I'll have to get a Honda! (*He quickly ties* GRANNY *up, takes away her blanket, ice pack, shawl and glasses, and pushes her under table. Then he sits down in easy chair, wraps blanket around his legs, and puts on shawl, glasses and ice pack. He calls in falsetto.*) Come i-i-i-n-n! (RED *enters.*)

RED: Good morning, Grandmother. Since you weren't feeling well, I brought you some goodies.

WOLF (*Falsetto*): Oh, you are such a thoughtful child! Come closer, so I can get a better look at you.

RED: Yes, Grandma. (RED *takes a step toward* WOLF *and starts to put basket down on table, which moves.* WOLF *quickly wiggles around in chair.*) Say, you sure are restless today!

WOLF: It's this new-fangled vibrating chair. Shakes the whole house!

RED: Oh, you have a new chair?

WOLF: Yes, come closer and look at it. It adjusts into a desk, a baby bed, or a hat rack. And in the summer it converts into an easy-haul camper.

RED: That's great, Grandma. Let me try it.

WOLF: Sure! Come over here and sit close to Grandma and tell me all about what's in the basket.(*Table moves again*)

RED: Well, O.K., but I can't stay too long. I have to go home and help my mother bake cookies for the PTA.

WOLF: If you'll come a step closer, you won't be here very long at all. (*Smiles at audience.*)

RED (*Stepping closer*): My, Grandma, what big eyes you have!

WOLF (*Winking at audience*): All the better to keep an eye on your basket with, my dear.

RED (*Stepping closer*): And what big teeth you have, Grandma!

WOLF (*Smacking lips and speaking in normal voice*): All the better to eat your goodies with, my dear! (*Grabs basket*) Give 'em here!

RED: Hey, you're not my grandma — you're the Wolf! (*Table wiggles violently. She pulls off tablecloth, revealing* GRANDMA.) There's my grandma! You big bully! (*Strikes at* WOLF, *who gets up and backs away hastily. Heavy pounding at door is heard.*)

BIG AL (*From offstage*): Open up in there! (*Breaks down door and falls into room with* JUNIOR)

FATHER-IN-LAW (*Entering*): Aha! I see we have come just in the nick of time!

RED: It's the Father-in-Law!

FATHER-IN-LAW: No! I am *not* the Father-in-Law. I

am a policeman disguised as the Father-in-Law on a special undercover assignment to capture the Big Bad Wolf. (*Takes off hat and turns down coat collar*) These are my partners, Lt. Monday and Sgt. Tuesday. (BIG AL *and* JUNIOR *also remove hats and turn down collars.* GRANDMA *squirms and tries to speak.* RED *hands basket to* JUNIOR *and unties* GRANDMA *as dialogue continues.*)

WOLF: But I'm clean! You've got nothing on me!

FATHER-IN-LAW: Oh, no? We have a 101 on you for bothering some kid called Peter; a 104 turned in by three pigs; and a 307 for disturbing the peace on nights when there's a full moon. (*Takes* WOLF *by arm*) Come on, let's go.

WOLF: Not so fast. I'm entitled to call my lawyer — and while we're waiting maybe Grandma will serve tea and *goodies!*

GRANDMA: I don't have any tea, but I could get out these goodies. (*To* JUNIOR, *who is still holding basket*) Give me the basket, Thursday — or whatever your name is. (JUNIOR *hands basket to* GRANDMA. *She puts her hands into it, and feels contents.* WOLF *moves closer, licking lips and rubbing hands together greedily.* FATHER-IN-LAW *still holds his arm.* GRANDMA *lifts cloth covering basket and takes a peek.*) Oh! These *are* goodies! (*Pulls out several 78 rpm records and reads labels*) Look! A Guy Lombardo waltz! And this one is Bing Crosby crooning "You Are My Sunshine"! And here's a real oldie but goodie — a Lawrence Welk polka recorded when he was only thirty-seven!

WOLF (*To audience*): These are goodies? (*Turns to* FATHER-IN-LAW *and holds out hands as if for handcuffs.*) Take me in, officer. Jail never looked so good! (*Quick curtain*)

THE END

Jack, the Beanstalk and Chicken

A fairy tale retold

Characters

NARRATOR
JACK
JACK'S MOTHER
W. C. FIELDSTON
CHICKEN
GIANT

SCENE 1

BEFORE RISE: NARRATOR *enters in front of curtain.*

NARRATOR: The story you are about to see concerns Jack and the Beanstalk. It takes place once upon a long time ago. The setting is the usual fairy tale place, wherever that is. The first scene opens as Jack, his mother, and their last remaining cow are facing the hardships of poverty together. (*Exits; curtains open*)

SETTING: *Kitchen in Jack's cottage.*

AT RISE: JACK'S MOTHER *is pacing.* JACK *is sitting at table.*

MOTHER: What are we going to do, Jack? The cupboard is bare, the icebox is empty, the garden isn't growing, and we're flat broke.

JACK: Set that to music and you'll have a country and western hit on your hands.

MOTHER: Don't be funny, boy. We're out of food and we're out of money.

JACK: I wouldn't worry, Mother. A fairy godmother will probably appear and turn an ordinary pumpkin into a beautiful, golden coach.

MOTHER: I'd rather have the pumpkin. (JACK *stands and mimics girl skipping.*)

JACK: Or maybe Little Red Riding Hood will come tripping up to the door with a basket of goodies.

MOTHER: Sit down! (*Checks* JACK's *forehead for fever*) Lack of food seems to be affecting your mind.

JACK: Well, a handsome prince could come along with a glass slipper, and —

MOTHER (*To audience*): I'm starving and he makes like Hans Christian Andersen.

JACK: I know! How about my taking the cow into town and trading her for something to eat?

MOTHER: Oh, no, you don't! I've heard that story before. You stay here, and *I'll* take the cow to town. (*Primping before mirror*) First I'd better change into something a little more fancy. You never can tell when I might meet a rich merchant who's looking for a good wife. (*Exits right*)

JACK: But, Mother, you've been saying that for ten years! (*He notices that* MOTHER *has left, and shrugs. There is a knock on door.*)

W. C. FIELDSTON (*From offstage*): Hello! (*He enters left. He speaks in manner of W. C. Fields.*) W. C. Fieldston here. Tell me, m' boy, is your mother home?

JACK: Yes, but she's in the other room getting ready to take our cow to town to sell.

W.C.: Cow? Sell a cow, you say?

JACK: Yes, so that we can have food.

W.C. (*To audience*): Suffering sciatica! My heart bleeds for this poor, starving child. (*To* JACK) Tell me, little fella, did your cow happen to graze next to that small, brown Jersey I saw across the street as I chanced upon your house?

JACK: That small, brown Jersey across the street *is* our cow.

W.C.: Your cow, you say? Too bad, too bad.

JACK: Why do you say that? She's a good cow.

W.C.: Well, now, the cow across the street has a classic case of moovitis. Yes, siree, a classic case, yes.

JACK: Moovitis? What's that?

W.C.: Tell me, m' boy, does the beast ever turn and cast its large brown eyes upon you and make a moo-ing sound?

JACK: Why, yes, all the time.

W.C.: Didn't I tell you so? What a pity — a classic case, yes. Only one thing can save her.

JACK: What's that?

W.C.: This. (*Takes large medicine bottle from pocket.*)

Wickery's Remedial Balm and Pharmaceutic. I was once embarked upon a mission of mercy in the Saharagobi Jungle with Dr. Benjamin Wickery, the world-famous dental surgeon. He taught me how to prevail upon the Appalandic cactus to yield its juices for science and medicine. I have bottled this excellent elixir, and am making it available to certain suitable persons, yes.

JACK: Oh?

W.C.: Yes, it's good for rheumatism, corns, and the heartbreak of psoriasis.

JACK: But how could that help our cow?

W.C.: Patience, boy, I'm getting to that. It also grows organic vegetables, removes bumper stickers, and cures moovitis.

JACK: Hey, that's just what we need!

W.C.: Unmistakably, m' boy, but this happens to be the very last bottle left in the whole entire world. (*Removes hat*) I couldn't part with it for any price. (*Replaces hat*)

JACK: Oh, well, we couldn't buy it anyway. We don't have any money.

W.C.: Ah-h-h, yes — no money. Tell you what, m' boy, my generosity overflows whenever I see a young lad in distress. I'm going to allow you to steal this great panacea, this elixir of the gods, for — say ... one cow. An offer I would not make even to my sainted mother. (*Removes hat*) May she rest in peace. (*Replaces hat*)

JACK: One cow! Hey, we don't have any money, but we do have a cow! It's a deal!

W.C.: Ah, yes, a wise and noble decision. (*He hands* JACK *bottle with flourish.*) I can see you are a boy of wit and distinction. (*Prepares to leave*) My regards to your dear mother. (*Tips hat and exits left*)

JACK: Oh, boy! The last bottle in the entire world and I was able to get it! (MOTHER *re-enters, wearing hat*)

MOTHER: What's all the yelling about?

JACK (*Holding up bottle*): A man just sold me this great medicine that will cure our cow of moovitis.

MOTHER: Sold? How could anybody sell you anything? We don't have any money. The only thing we have left is . . .

JACK *and* MOTHER (*Turning to audience; together*): The cow.

MOTHER: You ding-a-ling! (*Grabs bottle from* JACK) You traded our cow for this worthless bottle of junk (*Throws it out window*) that won't cure anything, for our cow that didn't have anything, that we couldn't cure anyway because you traded it! (*Aside to audience*) Did I say that right?

JACK: I'm sorry, Mother. (*Goes to window.*) It sounded like a good deal at the time. I guess I didn't think. (*Suddenly*) Hey! Look out there in the garden where you threw the bottle! Something is growing! (*Excitedly*) It's a beanstalk!

MOTHER: Let me see! (*She goes to window. Both appear to watch a beanstalk rising offstage. Sound of slide whistle on rising pitch is heard.*) How about that!

JACK: Wow! I'm going out to climb it and look for the goose that lays the golden eggs.

MOTHER: Wait, Jack . . . (*He exits.*) Oh, well, what harm can it do? They say travel broadens the mind; and there's nobody who needs that more than Jack. (*Curtain*)

*   *   *   *   *

SCENE 2

SETTING: *Room in Giant's castle, with a banner or tapestry hanging from stone wall, and throne-like chair. Everything is standard size except for large nest in one corner.*

AT RISE: CHICKEN *is sitting on nest.*

CHICKEN (*Smiling and flapping wings*):
Cluck, cluck, cluck, cluck-cu-duck.
Cluck, cluck, cluck, cluck-cu-duck.
(JACK *enters right and looks around without seeing* CHICKEN.)

JACK: This should be the Giant's castle!

CHICKEN: Hi, Jack! (JACK *freezes.*)

JACK (*Startled*): Who—who said that?

CHICKEN: Me, dodo, who else?

JACK: Oh, I'll bet you're the goose that lays golden eggs!

CHICKEN: Goose! Golden eggs? You've got to be kidding! I'm Chicken.

JACK: Chicken! Chicken? I suppose this means you don't lay golden eggs, either!

CHICKEN: You said it — no golden eggs. However, I

can whip up a mean omelet.

JACK: Hey, that's even better! I'm starved. In fact, I'll take you up on that right now. Let's make ourselves scarce before the Giant gets here. (*He reaches out to take* CHICKEN.)

CHICKEN: Touch me and I'll squawk!

JACK: So what? I'm not afraid. I can outrun a giant and outflap a chicken any day. Come on! (*Takes* CHICKEN *by wing and starts to exit.*)

CHICKEN (*Flapping wildly*): Squawk! Squawk! Ska-waak!

GIANT (*From offstage, speaking into megaphone in very loud, gruff voice*): Fee, fie, foe, fum! I smell the blood of an Englishman.

CHICKEN: You've had it, wise guy. You'd better let me go right now! (JACK *releases* CHICKEN *who struts to nest.*)

JACK: Something tells me this story is not going right. (GIANT *stomps in. He is of normal height.*)

GIANT (*Speaking through megaphone*): Fee, fie, foe, fum. Look out, Jack, here I come! (JACK *is about to run, but stops when he sees* GIANT.)

JACK: Hey, wait! You're not a Giant.

GIANT (*Without megaphone; pouting*): Oh, drat! You noticed!

JACK: Why do you go around using that bull-horn?

GIANT (*Whining*): How else can I scare people away? It's not easy when you're a tiny giant. People are supposed to run away when they hear me coming. You've spoiled everything!

JACK: Look, *I'm* not spoiling anything. I came up here

to get a goose that lays golden eggs and what do I find? A chicken!

CHICKEN (*Smiling*): Cluck, cluck, cluck, cluck, cu-duck!

GIANT: Well, she is a chicken, all right, but she does make a terrific omelet. Want to split one with me now?

JACK: Yes. I'm still starving.

MOTHER (*From offstage*): Yoo-hoo, Jack! Where are you? (*Enters right, panting*) Oh, there you are. Come on home!

JACK: Mother! You climbed the beanstalk, too?

MOTHER: Yes, I came to get you. You know that stuff that wouldn't cure anything, that you traded for a cow that didn't have anything, that you couldn't cure anyway because you traded it? (*Gasps for breath*)

JACK: Yes, Mother, I remember. It made the beanstalk grow.

MOTHER: It made *all* the fruits and vegetables in our garden grow, fast ... and they're selling faster. We're going to be rich. Forget all this golden-egg-wild-goose chase and get back down and help me!

JACK: O.K., Mother. Could Chicken come, too? She makes a great omelet.

MOTHER (*Studying* CHICKEN *skeptically*): Chicken? Sure, we could use another cook now that I'm going to be so busy.

CHICKEN (*Smiling and flapping wings*): Cluck, cluck, cluck, cluck cu-duck.

GIANT (*Using megaphone*): Say, Jack, you didn't introduce me to the lady!

JACK: Oh, Mother, may I present Giant? Giant, this is my mother.

MOTHER (*To* GIANT): Say, you're cute. But you sure don't look like a giant to me.

GIANT (*Without megaphone*): That's because I'm a tiny giant. But I'm no success as a giant. I don't frighten anybody.

MOTHER: You might make a good gardener. (*Primps hair and smiles*) Would you care to come down the beanstalk with us and help with the organically grown vegetables?

GIANT: I'll be happy to try — but I'm not very good at it.

JACK *and* MOTHER (*Together*): Why not?

GIANT: I don't have a green thumb — ho, ho, ho!

MOTHER: We're going to expand our vegetable business. We'll switch you to the advertising department. With that jolly laugh and green suit — we can use you in our commercials.

ALL (*Singing to the tune of "Good Things from the Garden," TV commercial jingle*):
> Climbing down the beanstalk,
> Going to our garden,
> Garden of the tiny —

GIANT (*Singing*):
> Ho, ho, ho!

ALL (*Singing*):
> Green giant. (*Curtain*)

THE END

The Tortoise and the Hare Hit the Road

A famous race with a new face ...

Characters

NARRATOR
FOX, *sly and crafty*
BEAR, *forgetful*
BLUE JAY, *a prizefighter who brags about himself in poems*
CHICKEN, *who is afraid the sky will fall*
HARE, *speedy but awkward*
LION, *the King of Beasts*
DOG, *loyal to King*
TORTOISE, *slow but steady*

SCENE 1

BEFORE RISE: NARRATOR *enters in front of curtain.*
NARRATOR: This fable was made up by a guy named Aesop so he could sit around telling stories like this and get out of doing hard work. This Aesop's fable is about the Great Race — the footfall 500 — be-

tween the Tortoise, or Turtle, and the Hare, or Rabbit. And, of course, all of you know that the Tortoise always wins that race. But, as our story opens, we find the Fox and Blue Jay about to change all that. (*Exits*)

SETTING: *Forest. A tree stump is at center.*
AT RISE: FOX *is sitting on stump, dejected.*

BEAR (*Entering, dressed as Smokey the Bear, with sign reading* ONLY YOU CAN PREVENT FOREST FIRES *in his hand, and positioning himself to address* FOX): Only you can prevent ... ah-h ... only you can prevent ... ah-h ... prevent ...
FOX (*Without looking up*): Forest fires.
BEAR: Forest fires! Forest fires! If I can learn to get that right, I might be on television! Forest fires. . . . (*Mumbles "forest fires" several times as he exits*)
FOX: What a rotten, crummy forest! Me, the Fox, slyest and craftiest of all the inhabitants herein — and I'm practically flat broke!
BLUE JAY (*Entering, doing what is supposed to be jogging, but always looks more like a smooth, strutting dance step with some shadow-boxing thrown in; with each jab of his fist he is mouthing a barely audible "pow" in a slow, blues style*): Oh, I am the best! I am number one! (*Stops at center stage*) I have a poem (*Recites*):
     I am the greatest;
     I sting like a bee.

I move like a butterfly;
Look out for me!

Fox: Yeah, yeah — take another lap.

Blue Jay (*Continuing rhythmic jog across stage to opposite exit*): Oh, I am the best! I am number one! (*Exits*)

Fox: Surely there must be some way I can get my hands — er, paws — on some good, hard cash! (*Shifts position, scratches head, thinking*)

Blue Jay (*Entering as before*):
I am the greatest;
I sting like a bee.
I move like a butterfly —

Fox (*Interrupting*): Just cool it, Blue Jay, will you? You can be the greatest when the press is here. Right now we have money problems.

Bear (*Entering and addressing* Blue Jay): Only you can prevent ... ah-h ... only you can prevent ... ah-h ... prevent ... What is it?

Fox: Forest fires.

Bear: Forest fires! That's it! Forest fires! Now, why can't I get that right? I'll never get to be on TV. (*Exits, muttering*) Forest fires, forest fires, forest fires ...

Blue Jay: Money problems? We always have money problems. Why didn't you train me to be a runner (*Runs in place*) instead of a *great* fighter? (*Boxes, mouthing "pow, pow, pow," with smooth, rhythmic motions*) Then I could enter the Great Race and beat both the Rabbit and the Turtle.

Fox (*Perking up*): The Tortoise and the Hare? Are

they still running that race?

BLUE JAY: Yeah, but, as usual, nobody's paying much attention. What they need is new blood — me! The greatest! Listen, I have a poem (*Recites*):
> I can beat the Hare,
> With room to spare!

Fox: Hey, that's it! The Great Race! We can pick up a bundle.

BLUE JAY: You really want me to race? I was kidding. I thought I was training to be a fighter.

Fox: Why not? Sure, why not? Every year that reckless Rabbit races the Turtle, and every year he speeds out ahead, then takes a nap and loses, right?

BLUE JAY: Right, but —

Fox: Now, nobody, I mean, nobody, in his right mind anywhere in this forest will bet on the Rabbit to win, right?

BLUE JAY: Right, but —

Fox: Now just suppose that the Rabbit had some *real* competition — someone that would scare him into running fast and *not* taking a nap. That way our forest friends would bet on him to win — right?

BLUE JAY: Right, but —

Fox: "Right, but" nothing! It will work. Now, listen: I want you to go around the forest bragging about how you can beat the Rabbit — that shouldn't be too hard for you — so that we can pick up a few bets and win some money, right?

BLUE JAY: Right, but . . . (*Brightening*) Money? Right!

Fox: Compose a few more poem predictions about being the winner and by how much, and I'll meet you later at the starting point.

BLUE JAY (*Exchanging soul hand-slaps with* FOX *and heading for exit, reciting*):

> Oh, I am the greatest;
> I sting like a bee. (*Exits*)

FOX: That's step one. Now for a clever step two of a sly and, pardon the expression, "foxy" plan. (*Contemplates, rubbing chin and scratching head*)

BEAR (*Entering*): Only you can prevent —

FOX (*Impatiently*): Will you go practice somewhere else?

BEAR: Well, sure, but I only want to keep trying so I can get it right and be on TV. (*Exits, mumbling*) Gee, whiz. Practice is supposed to make perfect.

FOX (*Continuing to think*): Hmm-m-m! Uh-huh-h-h! Yes! (*Calls*) Chicken! Hey, Chicken!

CHICKEN (*Entering hurriedly and nervously*): Yes? Yes, sir, Mr. Fox? You called? (*Looks up*) Ooops! (*Returns quickly to exit and stands so only head is showing*) Oh, it's so open out there! (*Still looking up*) The sky might fall!

FOX: The sky is not going to fall!

CHICKEN: Oh, but there's so much space, and you know how I hate to be where so much space is showing, because the sky might fall and there I would be, and —

FOX: C'm'ere!

CHICKEN (*Hurrying in, with umbrella, and standing meekly next to* FOX): Yes, sir, Mr. Fox. (*Opens umbrella and hovers underneath it.*)

FOX: Look, Chicken, I want —

CHICKEN: Please, Mr. Fox, my name is not "Chicken."
I am *a chicken* and my name is —

Fox: Look, Chicken.

CHICKEN (*Quickly*): I'm looking.

Fox: I need to make a bundle, and you're going to
help me.

CHICKEN (*Leaning closer*): I'm helping.

Fox: The next Great Race between the Tortoise and
the Hare is coming up soon, and I'm going to fix it
so the Rabbit will win. Get it?

CHICKEN: But I thought you just told that bragging
Blue Jay he could win!

Fox: Chicken, if you know what's good for you, you
didn't hear me tell that Jay a single, solitary word.

CHICKEN (*Feigning innocence*): Did you say something?

Fox: Just now — to the Blue Jay.

CHICKEN: I didn't hear anything.

Fox: Right... Now, here's the plan. That bird-brained
Blue Jay can talk up a storm, but at running, he
couldn't beat a lame snail. In this race with the Tortoise and the Hare, the Bunny, as usual, will jump
out ahead, then take a snooze in that flower patch
about 200 yards from the finish. I want you to go
down to that spot, and —

CHICKEN: Oh, but that flower patch has a large KEEP
OUT sign, and I don't think that I should be —

Fox: When I'm telling the plan, you be quiet!

CHICKEN: I'm quiet.

Fox: You go down to the flower patch with some eggs
all decorated like Easter eggs, see. And when the

Hare comes, you pop out and say to him, "Surprise! You, Noble Rabbit, have been named Honorary Easter Bunny, and must deliver these eggs to the village!" Since the finish line is between there and the village, he'll grab the eggs and trot off down the road, and that way he'll win the race.

CHICKEN: Easter Bunny! Deliver Easter eggs! Really, the whole idea is so preposterous he'll never fall for it.

FOX: That harebrained Hare will believe anything.

CHICKEN: Come on — the Rabbit has more sense than that.

FOX (*Strongly*): I like the idea!

CHICKEN: So do I.

FOX: Now, go get busy coloring those eggs (CHICKEN *moves toward exit*), or I'll bring the sky down on you.

CHICKEN (*Running toward exit*): Don't say that! (*Holding umbrella closer, exits*)

FOX: Now to lunch on a few sweet grapes and prepare for the Great Race. (*Exits; curtain.*)

*   *   *   *   *

SCENE 2

BEFORE RISE: NARRATOR *enters in front of curtain.*

NARRATOR: Scene One is finished and the stage is now prepared for the climactic second, and concluding, scene. But, before we continue, I shall recapitulate the proceedings of Scene 1, all of which hinge on two major factors: One, the Fox and the Blue Jay want money; and, two, it is about time for the annual Great Race between the Tortoise, or Turtle, and the Hare, or Rabbit. But, alas, this event has become so predictable that no one cares if they race or not. Taking advantage of the situation, the sly Fox will enter his protegé, the Blue Jay, in what has formerly been a "grudge duel." Now, anyone with a knack for probability and chance can link these events and, with a hot tip, pick up a bundle. As we begin Scene Two, we await the answers to these questions: Who will win the race? If the Jay is Number One, a car rental Number Two, what does that leave for Number Three? It is easy for the Fox to outfox the chicken Chicken, but how much longer can he bear the Bear? What really does hold up the sky? And, last but certainly not least, just what is the difference between a tortoise and a turtle? Or, for that matter, a rabbit and a hare? (*Begins to exit*) Or a terrapin and a bunny? Or a bison and a buffalo? Or a (*Exits*) pony and a horse? Or . . . (*Sticks head back onstage*) let Scene Two begin! (*Exits*)

SETTING: *Same as Scene 1, except stump is removed and replaced with sign reading* START *on one side and* FINISH *on the other. A throne is at one side.*

AT RISE: HARE, *a bounding bundle of awkward energy, is practicing fast starts.* BEAR, *holding sign, is watching.* DOG *is impatiently pacing at starting point and glancing at watch.* FOX *is sitting in a relaxed position downstage while* CHICKEN *holds um-*

brella over them both. LION *enters and all turn, or, if seated, stand and bow.*

ALL (*Ad lib*): It's the King! Hail the King! Good afternoon, Your Majesty. (*Etc.*)

LION: Is he here yet? That Super-Ego Blue Jay I've been hearing so much about?

DOG: No, Your Majesty, and it's almost time for the race. I think maybe it was all brag and he won't show. (FOX *returns to seated position downstage.*)

LION (*Disappointed*): Oh? Too bad. I was looking forward to it. It's such a bore having the Turtle win year after year.

HARE (*Speaking, as he moves, in rapid, staccato sentences, with pauses, drawing out some sounds*): Luck! That's what it's been, luck! Luck-luck-luck! I can run fast! Fast, you hear, fast! Watch how I do this fast start! (*Starts quickly, but stumbles*)

CHICKEN: Oh, you are such a dud! Once a loser, always a loser.

HARE: What do you know, Chicken! (*Mimics*) The sky is falling! The sky is falling!

CHICKEN (*Huddling under umbrella*): Don't say that!

DOG: Now, now. We are here for the race. Let's not spoil it with bickering.

CHICKEN: All right, but I still say he's a loser. Don't take my word for it, though. There are others here. What do you think, Smokey?

BEAR: Me? Well, I think that only you can prevent . . . ah, prevent . . . ah . . .

ALL (*Together*): Forest fires!

BEAR: Right! Forest fires! I'll never get on TV at this rate!

HARE: Say what you like. This year I will win. I am ready-ready-ready. You hear? Ready! See these moves? See? (*Moves about quickly but not gracefully*)

LION: Tell us, Fox . . . You know Blue Jay. Is he really that good?

BLUE JAY (*Enters, dancing around as in Scene 1*): Am I good? No. Am I better? No. Am I the best? No! Because I'm better than the best! Yes! I am the greatest! I am number one!

HARE: Oh, no! Now I get it. I know what he'll do — he'll fly! He's a *bird,* isn't he? Huh? Isn't he? He'll fly! That's not fair! Not fair at all! This race is for running, not flying! I protest! Protest-protest-protest!

BLUE JAY: I have a prediction for you, Rabbit — a poem — (*Recites*):

> It is true I will fly,
> But not in the air.
> My feet will leave prints,
> Right over the Hare!

HARE: No, you won't. I am fast! I can beat you. I can-I can-I can! So . . . in the past I slept a few times. That's not my fault. The Tortoise has just been lucky. That's all — lucky-lucky-lucky!

FOX (*Who has been unmoved by all that has taken place until now*): I think maybe the Rabbit is right. (*Stands, crosses to* RABBIT, *and looks him over*) He sure looks quick to me.

RABBIT (*Darting here and there*): I am, I am!

Fox: And look here — that is a Blue Jay. Is there something about the name that makes you think about speed? No! We sing the blues — we jaywalk ... but, on the other hand, when we really think about speed, we say, "As fast as a greased rabbit."

CHICKEN: Greased rabbit? I haven't heard that —

Fox (*Threateningly*): It's a well-known saying!

CHICKEN (*Quickly*): Since yesterday.

LION (*Standing*): I think I'll place my bet on the —

DOG: Sire ... please. (*Indicates that they should step aside to talk. They move downstage.*) Sire, if that sly Fox is saying the Rabbit will win, you'd better bet on the Blue Jay.

LION: Oh? You think the Fox is up to his cunning tricks again, do you?

Fox (*Aside, to* CHICKEN): Step out there and bet on the Rabbit to win.

CHICKEN: Me? But I don't have any money, and besides, betting is not something I approve of doing.

Fox: Now!

CHICKEN (*Loudly*): I'm placing my money on the Hare. Who will give me odds?

DOG: I'll take an even twenty on the Blue Jay.

LION: And I'll make it fifty for the Jay to win!

Fox: All right, and I'll hold the stakes. First your money. (*Steps center and takes* DOG's *and* LION's *money, then moves to* CHICKEN) And now yours.

CHICKEN (*Pulling* Fox *aside*): But I *told* you I don't have any money!

Fox: Just consider it a loan.

CHICKEN: But I said I don't have any.

FOX: You'll get it back —

CHICKEN: But, I don't have any.

FOX: Next time the *sky falls.*

CHICKEN (*Cowering*): Don't say that!

FOX: Then don't hold out on the Fox.

CHICKEN: Well (*Reaching into purse*), I do happen to have a small amount of cash — sort of a nest egg — that I was saving for a (*Peeks out from under umbrella at the sky*) . . . a rainy day. (*Ducks back under and reluctantly hands money to* FOX.)

FOX (*Taking it with a smile*): When the race is over, we'll be showered with greenbacks. (*Moves to* BEAR) And how about the fur-trimmed fearless firefighter? Care to make a small wager?

BEAR: Ah, no. Not really. You see, I'm not a betting person. In fact, the only, ah, money I have is this five. (*Holds up bill*)

FOX (*Snatching money*): And five big ones for the Stalwart Smoke Stomper. (BEAR *stands perplexed.*)

LION (*Moving to throne*): Let the race begin!

HARE (*Miffed at those betting against him*): All of you are making a mistake — a big mistake. I am ready-ready-ready! (*Gets on mark and practices starts*)

BLUE JAY: They know a winner when they see one, and I am a winner! I am the greatest! (*Moves to starting line and sways rhythmically*)

TORTOISE (*Entering, moving very, very slowly — as if in a slow-motion film — and speaking with slow drawl*): Well, here I am, yep. All set for another Great Race with the Hare.

LION: The Tortoise! We forgot all about the Tortoise!

BLUE JAY: You're too late. This year the Hare is going to be beaten by the greatest: Me — number one! Matinee Blue Jay!

HARE: Oh, no! No-no-no! This year I'm going to win! You hear? Win-win-win!

LION (*To* DOG): We forgot all about the Tortoise. Now what do we do?

DOG: Well, he is last year's winner.

TORTOISE: Yep, and the year before that, and the year before that, and the year before that, and the year —

HARE: Rub it in! That's it — just go ahead and rub it in! But, when I beat that bragging bird-brain you'll see what a winner I am! You'll see!

TORTOISE: Well, that's fine with me, yep. But when will you beat me?

DOG: He has a point. After all, the Tortoise is the champ. And if either of you is to become the next champion, then you must defeat the present champion.

BLUE JAY: Let him run — er, enter. I am the greatest! When I beat both of them, then I will be the greatest champion!

HARE: Ha! We'll see about that! We'll see!

LION: Racers to the starting line.

HARE (*Squatting for quick start and mumbling*): Win-win-win-win . . .

BLUE JAY (*Strutting to line*): First I have a prediction — a poem — about who will win. (*Clears throat*)
>The Jay will be a winner
>And back in his nest for dinner.

DOG: All right, here we go. (TORTOISE *moves to line also.*) Ready . . .

ALL (*Repeating*): Ready!

DOG: Steady . . .

ALL (*Repeating*): Steady!

DOG: Go! Go! Go! (*All yell encouraging words as* HARE *speeds out right exit, followed by the dancelike moves of* BLUE JAY, *and last by very, very slow, lumbering* TORTOISE.)

FOX (*Aside to* CHICKEN): O.K., Chicken, get on down to where you have those Easter eggs ready and do your stuff.

CHICKEN: Are you really quite sure this will work? After all, the —

FOX (*Sharply*): Hey!

CHICKEN: I'm going! (*Exits.* LION, BEAR, *and* DOG *move upstage and stand with backs to audience, as though watching the runners move in a semicircle from right to left.*)

LION: I can't see the bird anymore.

DOG: I can't see the Hare.

BEAR: I can see — smoke! Smoke! Oh, boy! I get to go and stamp out a campfire. (*Exits in a rush*)

DOG (*As all continue to follow the imaginary movement of the racers*): Hey, someone's coming!

LION: It's the Rabbit!

DOG: No, it's the Blue Jay!

BEAR (*Entering*): No, it's me. Remember, only you can prevent forest fires. Hey! I said it right! I said it right! Television, here I come! (*Exits*)

TORTOISE (*Entering left*): Well, here I am — winning again. (*Moves to finish line*) Yep, guess I'm still the champion.

LION: Oh, no!

DOG: It can't be!

FOX: I'm dreaming! I have to be dreaming!

LION: What happened to the Blue Jay?

DOG: What happened to the Hare?

FOX: Wait till I get my hands — er, paws — on that Chicken!

TORTOISE: The Hare? Well, the last I saw of him he was zipping down the shortcut to the village carrying a basket of Easter eggs. The Chicken was high-stepping along right behind him, yelling something like, "Stop! Stop! You're going the wrong way!" And you know, it sounded as if that Hare said he had to deliver the eggs! I think the sun got to him, yep.

LION: What happened to the Blue Jay?

BLUE JAY (*Entering, swaggering as before, and counting a large roll of bills*): Fifty-seven, fifty-eight, fifty-nine ... I would have been here sooner, but I, number one, the greatest, had to stop and pick up a small wager I made on the Turtle to win. Friends, a poem:

> When I said I was the greatest,
> I did not say at what.
> Sometimes great is getting,
> And getting's what I've got!

(*Quick curtain*)

THE END

Meet Dr. Frankenstein

A group of ghouls . . .

Characters

DR. FRANKENSTEIN, *evil scientific genius*
IGOR, *his hunchbacked assistant, unable to speak*
WOLFMAN, *hairy-faced werewolf*
DRACULA, *the Count of Transylvania*
TOMBSTONE, *who is looking for a grave*
VAMPIRA, *siren who wants to be alone*
HAPPY MEDIUM, *fortune-teller*
BOY
GIRL
OTHER CHILDREN, *extras*

TIME: *Late at night.*
SETTING: *Sinister, gloomy room in a haunted house belonging to Dr. Frankenstein.*
AT RISE: *Sounds of wind, thunder and lightning are heard from offstage. Door creaks as* DR. FRANKENSTEIN *enters, taking off coat and gloves.*

DR. FRANKENSTEIN (*Calling*): Igor! Igor! (IGOR *en-*

ters, *walking with a loping gait, hunched over slightly.*) What a terrible, dark and stormy night! (*They look out window.*) Beautiful, is it not?

IGOR: (*Capers around giving a grunting laugh*)

DR. FRANKENSTEIN: Tell me, Igor (*Handing him coat and gloves*), have any of my guests arrived yet?

IGOR: (*Shakes head and laughs while hanging up coat*)

DR. FRANKENSTEIN: No? This is most unusual! My invitation specifically read, "Twelve o'clock midnight." (*Looks at pocket watch*) This foolish daylight saving time! It has everybody confused! (*Knock is heard.* IGOR *starts toward door, but before he can reach it* DRACULA *steps in quickly, with his arms above his head, holding his cape like wings.*)

DRACULA: Good e-e-e-evening!

DR. FRANKENSTEIN: Ah, Count Dracula, I'm so pleased that you could come. (*Extends hand*)

DRACULA (*Clicking heels, bowing slightly, then taking outstretched hand and examining it with interest, licking lips*): My pleasure. (*Leers at audience*) You are like a relative to me. A *blood* relative. (*Raises arms, lifting cape, and lunges at* DR. FRANKENSTEIN'S *neck, baring his teeth.* DR. FRANKENSTEIN *quickly backs away.*)

DR. FRANKENSTEIN: No, no — stop. I gave at the office. The Red Cross office, that is.

IGOR: (*Laughs and moves behind* DRACULA *to take his cape as a butler would do*)

DRACULA (*Turning to look at* IGOR, *then speaking to* DR. FRANKENSTEIN): I see you are still experimenting, Doctor.

DR. FRANKENSTEIN: Oh, no! Igor is not an experiment. He is my associate. (IGOR *reaches for* DRACULA's *cape.*) No, Igor, no! (*Slaps at* IGOR's *arms and back*) Down! Down! Count Dracula never removes his cape.

IGOR: (*Laughs and lopes to opposite side of stage*)

DRACULA (*Smoothing cape; menacingly*): Your note said to come at midnight. You mentioned there would be *others.* (*Looks around room*)

DR. FRANKENSTEIN: Yes. (*Checks watch again*) I fail to comprehend why they are not here! (*Suddenly* WOLFMAN *rushes in through window, snarling and pawing the air with his hands. He moves toward* DRACULA.)

DRACULA (*Raising arm imperiously*): Stop, stop, you beast! One step nearer and I'll bite your neck.

WOLFMAN (*Dropping his menacing act; apologetically*): Ah, heck. Gee whiz! Weren't you scared, huh? Didn't I frighten anyone? (*Looks around*) How about you, Doctor? Were you scared? Huh?

DR. FRANKENSTEIN (*Condescendingly*): It was an impressive try, Wolfman.

WOLFMAN (*To* IGOR): How about you? Were you scared?

IGOR: (*Cavorts about, clapping hands and emitting grunting laugh*)

WOLFMAN (*Cringing and drawing away from* IGOR): I see you're still working on experiments in that basement laboratory of yours, Doctor. (*From off-stage, voice of* TOMBSTONE *is heard, speaking in a slow, quavering, hollow monotone.*)

TOMBSTONE (*Off*): Hark! Death is calling! The grave seeks its victim! Come, your fate awaits!

DR. FRANKENSTEIN: Igor, Tombstone has arrived! (IGOR *opens door.*)

TOMBSTONE (*Entering slowly*): Here I am: the fitting memorial for the poor remains of some dear, departed soul. You have someone who needs me? A friend? A relative?

DR. FRANKENSTEIN (*Moving closer to shake hands*): Tombstone, I'm so happy you could come. (*No hand is available, leaving* DR. FRANKENSTEIN *in an awkward position.*)

TOMBSTONE: Just pat my R.I.P. (DR. FRANKENSTEIN *does so.*) Ah-h-h-h, you have such a clammy touch! (DR. FRANKENSTEIN *quickly removes his hand.*) Tell me, Dr. Frankenstein, you must have someone *lying* around here who could use me. (*Turns to face* IGOR) Him, perhaps.

DR. FRANKENSTEIN: No, Tombstone, that is Igor, my assistant. Say hello, Igor.

IGOR: (*Cavorts and emits grunting laugh*)

TOMBSTONE: Your assistant? (*Looks again*) Yes, parts of him look very familiar.

DR. FRANKENSTEIN (*Continuing with introductions*): I believe you know Count Dracula and Wolfman. (DRACULA *gives a slight bow and a click of heels.* WOLFMAN *snarls.*)

TOMBSTONE: Yes, I know them very well. They send a lot of customers my way. Now explain why you invited us here.

DR. FRANKENSTEIN: Patience, my dear Tombstone,

patience. There are still more to come, and besides (*Looks at watch*), it is not yet midnight — or it might be after midnight. With all these time changes, how is anybody to know?

TOMBSTONE: Body? Did you say body?

DR. FRANKENSTEIN (*Holding up watch*): No, I was referring to this confounded daylight saving time! I hate it!

TOMBSTONE: I hate any kind of daylight!

HAPPY MEDIUM (*From offstage in cackling voice*): Heh, heh, heh! (*Throws open door*) Don't be waiting for me, dearies. (*Steps inside, followed by* VAMPIRA) We're both (*Holds up crystal ball*) here and my crystal ball says we're right on time.

DRACULA: How would you know? That crystal ball is as worthless as a piece of rock.

TOMBSTONE (*Offended*): Please! Mind your metaphors.

DR. FRANKENSTEIN: Gentlemen and ladies — let us not deal in frivolities. We are not here to trade insults. We have a very serious matter to discuss. (*To* HAPPY MEDIUM *and* VAMPIRA) Please come in and make yourselves at home.

VAMPIRA (*Slinking to far corner*): I vant to be alone.

TOMBSTONE: Alone? Did you say *alone?* I have just the place for you.

IGOR: (*Begins grunting laugh.* VAMPIRA *turns her head and ignores them.*)

DR. FRANKENSTEIN: We are all here now. (*Holds up hands for attention*) Please listen. Each of us in this room faces a dire situation: No one is frightened of us anymore. (*All protest at once, loudly repeating following lines until* Dr. Frankenstein *quiets them.*)

Dracula: Lies, all lies!

Igor: (*Lopes around, shaking head, making angry sounds*)

Wolfman: (*Growls and snarls*)

Tombstone: No, no, it is not true!

Happy Medium: You're wrong, wrong, you hear! My crystal ball says you're wrong!

Dr. Frankenstein (*Shouting*): Cease and desist this obnoxious noise! (*All become quiet.*) Protest all you like, but deep down you know it is true! No one is frightened of us anymore. (*He looks at each of them in turn.*) Well?

Tombstone: I like the way you say, "Deep down."

Dr. Frankenstein (*Pointing to* Wolfman): When was the last time someone screamed in terror and fled for his life when you ravaged the countryside?

Wolfman: Oh, drat. I might as well tell you. Gee whiz. Since they started showing late movies on television it's very seldom anybody ever comes out at night. But ... but, I did scare an old lady in the park the other day during lunch. Of course (*Kicks at floor boyishly*), it was only because she thought I was a dog, trying to eat her tuna fish sandwich. And I don't even like tuna fish!

Dr. Frankenstein (*To* Dracula): And how about you, my dear Count? When last did you startle and terrify someone?

Dracula: Much too long. Much too long! Some

comedian *imitates* me on television commercials, and now, every time I speak, people laugh. Can you imagine? They laugh! I hope they laugh to death. (*Pauses and looks at audience*) Laugh to death? (*Smiles*) I like it! I like it!

DR. FRANKENSTEIN (*To* TOMBSTONE): And how about you, Tombstone? Do people cower and gasp in terror when you loom up in the dark of night?

TOMBSTONE: No, they don't. It's most degrading. They yell things like, "Hey, buddy, don't you ever get tired of being taken for granite?" Then they laugh ... gales and gales of jeering laughter. I cannot stand it anymore. (*Sobs*)

DR. FRANKENSTEIN: There, there. (*Comforts* TOMB-STONE) Things may look more gloomy tomorrow. (*Turns to* HAPPY MEDIUM) When you predict the future, Happy Medium, do people believe? Do they pay you extra when you offer a more promising future?

HAPPY MEDIUM: I guess I might as well confess. Business is off. I don't have any customers. These days, when I offer to look into the crystal ball and tell people their future, they say, "Forget it. I saw that routine on television last week." And then they walk away.

DR. FRANKENSTEIN: And therein, my fellow monsters, lies our problem: Television! (*To* WOLFMAN) It keeps people home on dark nights. (*To* DRACULA) It depicts you as a joke. (*To* TOMBSTONE) You as a silly superstition. (*To* HAPPY MEDIUM) And you as a meddlesome old woman who *guesses* at the future!

HAPPY MEDIUM (*Heatedly*): Meddlesome old woman? Guesses at the future?

DRACULA (*To audience*): Well, perhaps there is some truth in television, after all!

DR. FRANKENSTEIN (*Ignoring* DRACULA): And even I, Dr. Frankenstein, the great evil genius, creator of the world's most demonic monster! They show me as a simple cartoon madman, whose monster goes around helping others, like (*With disgust*) a Boy Scout. Revolting! (*Turns to* VAMPIRA) And Vampira, our beautiful and deadly Vampira, they show as a housewife with ring-around-the-collar.

VAMPIRA: I just vant to be alone.

DR. FRANKENSTEIN: Needless to say, if television continues to influence people, we will all be alone — very much alone!

DRACULA: Yes! I wish they would do away with television and just have movies. They knew how to show me as a menace.

TOMBSTONE: Right! And people had to *walk* home in the *dark* after the movies. (*Laughs wickedly*)

WOLFMAN: Gee, whiz . . . I just wish they would not show so many commercials with men wearing beards and moustaches and long hair. It gives me a good image.

DR. FRANKENSTEIN: Then what is our solution to be? What is our path out of this predicament?

HAPPY MEDIUM: Let me look into the crystal ball and find out.

DRACULA: Put away that worthless piece of junk and help us think. (*A knock is heard.*)

TOMBSTONE: Hark! Someone is coming in.

DR. FRANKENSTEIN: Shh! Keep still! Don't move! (*All grow quiet and stand motionless.*)

BOY (*Opening door, which creaks; timidly*): Hello? (*Enters, followed by* GIRL) Anyone home?

GIRL: I sure hope the owner doesn't mind. It's raining too hard to stay outdoors. (*Calling*) Come on, everybody. (OTHER CHILDREN *enter cautiously.*)

BOY (*Seeing* TOMBSTONE; *frightened*): Hey! What is this place, anyway?

GIRL (*Seeing* DRACULA): Look! Dracula! (*Frightened*) He looks real enough to bite me. (*Nervously*) I'm scared. Look at all these monsters!

BOY: That's what it is — a wax museum of monsters. (*Points to* DR. FRANKENSTEIN) Dr. Frankenstein! I saw the movie on the late show the other night in which he made his terrible monster. (*Alarmed*) It was really scary!

GIRL: That werewolf gives me the shivers.

BOY: This is sure a terrifying wax museum. I'd like to come back and see the exhibits — only in broad daylight.

GIRL: Me, too. Right now, let's get out of here. I'd rather be outside — storm or no storm. (*Starts for door*)

OTHER CHILDREN (*Ad lib*): I'm leaving! This place gives me the creeps! It's too scary! (*Etc.* GIRL, BOY *and* OTHER CHILDREN *exit.*)

DR. FRANKENSTEIN: Did you hear that? He said my monster was terrible!

WOLFMAN: And I gave them the shivers. Gee whiz!

(*Snarls a little*) Just like old times!

DRACULA: The girl thought I would bite her neck. I like it! I like it!

HAPPY MEDIUM: They thought they were in a wax museum. Imagine that — a wax museum. The boy said he would come back when we're open. I wonder if he would? (*Looks at crystal ball with puzzled expression*)

VAMPIRA (*From her corner*): Do you think people would *pay* to see us?

DR. FRANKENSTEIN: That's the answer! Turn this ordinary haunted house into a wax museum of horrors. People won't watch television anymore.

TOMBSTONE: We could charge admission. Frighten people and make money, too.

DRACULA: I could buy a new old castle in Transylvania. I like it! I like it!

WOLFMAN: I could sell tickets . . . That is, if there's a full moon.

HAPPY MEDIUM: I could set up a booth and tell fortunes to the people waiting in line.

DR. FRANKENSTEIN: I can give guided tours of my laboratory. And Igor can sell souvenirs. (*Chuckles wickedly*)

VAMPIRA: Suddenly I don't vant to be alone anymore. (*Crosses center*)

DRACULA: I like it! I like it! (*All move about, rearranging furniture and talking excitedly.*)

IGOR: (*Prances to front of stage, with grunting laugh, and holds up sign reading* THE END. *Curtain*)

THE END

Curses! Foiled Again!

A melodrama to leave you speechless

Characters

TWO NARRATORS
NELL TRUEHART, *the heroine*
BRUCE GOODGUY, *the hero*
NASTY COLFAX, *the villain*
OLIVER BADGE, *the sheriff*
LADIES *of the Friendly Gables Church Auxiliary and Helping Hand Society*

SCENE 1

BEFORE RISE: TWO NARRATORS *enter in front of curtain and take places behind podiums downstage.*
1ST NARRATOR: This is a melodrama.
PIANO: *Plays arpeggio. Curtain opens.*

TIME: *Long ago.*
SETTING: *Outdoors in Friendly Gables, a small town with many trees, church steeple and picket fence. There is a piano on or in front of stage.*
AT RISE: *Stage is empty.*

1ST NARRATOR: Our story takes place in the quaint and charming little village of Friendly Gables.

2ND NARRATOR: Yes, Friendly Gables, where the air is pure, life is simple, and the people are either extraordinarily good or extraordinarily bad. All it takes is a good story to tell the difference.

1ST NARRATOR: This particular graphic tale concerns Nell Truehart, the sweet and innocent heroine.

PIANO: *Plays "Hearts and Flowers" or other romantic theme.*

NELL (*Entering, batting eyes shyly and curtsying demurely; in sweet tone*): Ahhh! (*Exits*)

2ND NARRATOR: And the evil and sinister villain, Nasturnium Colfax.

PIANO: *Plays sinister theme.*

NASTY (*Entering, smiling evilly at audience, twirling moustache; in menacing tone*): Ah-h-h-h-h! (*Raises and lowers eyebrows at audience and exits, with cape draped over arm.*)

1ST NARRATOR: The true-blue, always kind, courteous, obedient, do-a-good-deed-daily hero is Bruce Goodguy!

PIANO: *Plays "William Tell Overture."*

BRUCE (*Entering, with hands clasped above head, smiling; in happy tone*): Ah-h-h! (*Exits*)

2ND NARRATOR: And adding to the penetrating, pulsating pathos is the representative of law and order, truth and justice, courage and just plain grit, the sheriff of Friendly Gables, Oliver Badge.

PIANO: *Plays "I'm an Old Cowhand."*

OLIVER (*Entering shyly, touching brim of hat; modestly*): Aw-w-w!

1ST NARRATOR: To supply a little local color, we have the Ladies of the Friendly Gables Church Auxiliary and Helping Hand Society.

LADIES (*Entering from both sides, giggling and "buzzing" as if with gossip; in shocked tone, ad lib*): Ah! Ah! (*Etc. They continue to buzz.*)

2ND NARRATOR: As we move . . . (*Louder*) As we move . . . (*Still louder*) As we . . . (*To* LADIES) Ladies, please!

LADIES: *Become quiet and stand motionless.*

2ND NARRATOR: Thank you. (*To audience*) As we move into the thickening plot, we note that everyone in the quiet and peaceful little town of Friendly Gables loves our heroine, Nell.

NELL: *Enters and walks past* LADIES.

LADIES (*In friendly tone*): Ah-h-h! (*They greet* NELL *with smiles, pats and waves.*)

1ST NARRATOR: And Nell, of course, loves everyone in Friendly Gables. (NELL *stops near exit; as* LADIES *file past her and exit, she smiles and nods at each one cordially.*)

2ND NARRATOR: But especially she loves Bruce Goodguy, our stalwart hero.

BRUCE (*Entering, carrying ax; seeing* NELL): Ah-h-h!

NELL (*Happily*): Ah-h-h! (*They move center and hold hands.*)

1ST NARRATOR: But, alas! Our hero is a poor woodcutter who must work long, strenuous hours to provide for his poor, sick mother.

BRUCE (*Releasing* NELL'S *hands; resolutely*): Aha! (*Shoulders ax and marches offstage, waving to* NELL)

NELL (*Sobbing*): Ah! (*Runs after him*)

BRUCE (*Putting ax down, raising hand to stop her; warningly*): Ah! (*Exits without ax*)

2ND NARRATOR: Brave Bruce loves his work, and one day he will accumulate enough cash to enable him and our heroine to get married and live happily ever after.

PIANO: *Plays villain's theme.*

NASTY: *Enters and slinks down center.*

1ST NARRATOR: Meanwhile, enter the villain, Nasturnium Colfax, known to everyone, including his mother, as "Nasty."

NASTY (*Reacting with disgust to NARRATOR's comment*): Ah!

1ST NARRATOR: He is looking for a way to discredit poor Bruce forever and leave sweet Nell free to marry someone else, namely him!

NASTY (*Reacting with pleasure*): Ah-h-h-heh-heh-heh! (*Twirls moustache*)

2ND NARRATOR: Suddenly he spies our noble Bruce's ax. He knows his long-awaited opportunity has arrived.

NASTY (*Spying ax*): Aha! (*Moves to ax, picks it up, smiles diabolically at audience and exits. Curtain.*)

* * * * *

SCENE 2

BEFORE RISE: NARRATORS *continue.*

1ST NARRATOR (*Continuing with no pause between*

scenes): Now let us pause for a few seconds and take dramatic license to allow for the passage of several hours. We take up our story again early the next day. (*Curtain opens.*)

AT RISE: *Stage is empty. Ax has been returned to place where* BRUCE *left it.*
PIANO: *Plays light trill.*
2ND NARRATOR: As the good people of Friendly Gables arise to a brand-new morning, we are shocked to hear wails of suffering.
LADIES (*Entering a few at a time, some carrying branches of trees; mournfully or consolingly*): Augh-h-h! Ah-h-h.
1ST NARRATOR: Some diabolic evil-doer chopped down every tree in town while the unsuspecting citizens slept peacefully in their humble homes.
BRUCE (*Entering, walking swiftly to ax; surprised and puzzled*): Ah?
2ND NARRATOR: No one knows whom to suspect of such malicious malpractice, until circumstantial evidence points to our poor woodchopper (*Pointing with sweeping gesture at* BRUCE), Bruce Goodguy!
BRUCE (*Starting to exit; pointing to himself to indicate, "Who, me?"*): Eh?
LADIES (*Turning, pointing at* BRUCE; *accusingly*): Ah-ha! (*They stand at one side of stage, pointing.*)
1ST NARRATOR: Immediately the town's fine, law-upholding sheriff is summoned.
OLIVER (*Entering and putting handcuffs on* BRUCE; *chastisingly*): Ah-h-h!

2ND NARRATOR: Although he has strong reservations that the cleancut Bruce has performed such a dastardly deed, he must do his duty, and our luckless hero is escorted off to jail.

OLIVER: *Leads* BRUCE *toward exit.*

NELL (*Entering; shocked and upset*): Ah! (*She watches* BRUCE *and* OLIVER *exit.*)

2ND NARRATOR: Meanwhile, Nasty Colfax sees opportunity knocking and swiftly maneuvers to win over our lovely heroine. He consoles her in her hour of dire grief.

NASTY (*Entering, moving to* NELL *and patting her hand sympathetically*): Ah-h-h!

NELL: *Cries on his shoulder.*

1ST NARRATOR: Nasty's plan might have worked but for the simple truth that virtue and justice always triumph over evil.

2ND NARRATOR: Nell, even in the throes of depression, has enough presence of mind to note that the footwear of Nasty Colfax is coated with mud — telltale mire from certain humble lawns in the area — where trees once grew.

NASTY (*Shaking fist at* NARRATOR): Ah-h-h!

NELL (*Stepping back to look at* NASTY's *boots, pointing, then clapping back of hand to mouth; shocked*): Ah!

1ST NARRATOR: "You chopped down those trees!" Nell accuses, only to find herself at his villainous mercy.

NASTY (*Clutching* NELL's *throat with both hands; angrily*): Ar-r-r!

2ND NARRATOR: But Oliver Badge, the good and wise sheriff, suspecting treachery from the very beginning, has all along had unflagging confidence in our hero, Bruce Goodguy.

PIANO: *Plays "William Tell Overture."*

BRUCE (*Entering with* OLIVER, *pausing, then marching across stage and pulling* NASTY *away from* NELL; *triumphantly, as if to say, "Take that"*): Aha!

2ND NARRATOR: And together they catch Nasty red-handed.

OLIVER (*Putting handcuffs on* NASTY, *admonishing him with wagging finger*): Ah-h-h! (*He pulls* NASTY *offstage by collar.*)

LADIES (*Entering, seeing* NASTY, *and nodding righteously*): Ah-h-h!

1ST NARRATOR: So, in the end, Nasty Colfax gets his just deserts. Also, the Friendly Gables Church Auxiliary and Helping Hand Society decides to hold a quilting bee that will raise enough money to support Bruce's mother for the rest of her days.

LADIES (*Pantomiming sewing, humming*): Ah-h-hum-m-m-m-m.

2ND NARRATOR: And now Bruce and Nell can get married and live happily ever after.

BRUCE (*Moving to* NELL): Ah-h-h!

NELL (*Clasping his hands*): Ah-h-h-h.

LADIES (*Putting chins on clasped hands; sighing*): Ah-h-h-h!

OLIVER (*Entering with* NASTY; *bashfully*): Aw-w-w.

NASTY (*As if to say, "Foiled again"*): Ah!

1ST NARRATOR: And that, my good audience, is the end.

ALL (*Disappointed*): Aw-w-w! (*Curtain*)

THE END

Cinderella Finds Time

If the shoe fits . . .

Characters

NARRATOR
CINDERELLA
TWO STEPSISTERS
STEPMOTHER
FAIRY GODMOTHER
CLOCK
PRINCE
COURTIER
PAGE

SCENE 1

SETTING: *Kitchen in Stepmother's house.*
AT RISE: NARRATOR *enters and stands facing audience as he speaks.*

NARRATOR: This is the story of Cinderella, who, as you know, lives with her mean stepmother and her lazy stepsisters. While they are loafing around the castle or living it up at parties, poor Cinderella has to stay

54

home and carry out the trash, polish the armor, and make sure all the other household chores are done. As our play begins, the stepsisters have received invitations to attend the Grand Ball at the Palace. The Prince has just returned home from the wars, and everyone wants him to get married. Now, at last, the long-awaited day of the Ball has arrived. (1ST STEP-SISTER *enters, yawns, and slowly plods toward chair.*) So as I take my leave, we find the household in a state of breathless excitement. (*Exits.* 1ST STEP-SISTER *slumps motionless into kitchen chair, her head resting in her hand. She yawns and shifts her head to rest on other hand.*)

1ST STEPSISTER: Cinderella! Cinderella!

CINDERELLA (*Entering with broom, mop, feather duster, and so forth*): Yes, Stepsister?

1ST STEPSISTER: Shut the window. I can't stand to hear those birds sing.

CINDERELLA: I'll be glad to, Stepsister. (*Shuts window, then exits*)

1ST STEPSISTER: Cinderella! Cinderella!

CINDERELLA (*Entering*): Yes, Stepsister?

1ST STEPSISTER: Open the window. It's stuffy in here.

CINDERELLA: Why certainly, Stepsister. (*Opens window, then exits right, as* STEPMOTHER *enters left and sees* STEPSISTER *slouched in chair.*)

STEPMOTHER: Land sakes, girl! Why aren't you getting ready for the Grand Ball, where your natural beauty and charm will captivate the Prince, and he will marry you and you will live happily ever after?

1st Stepsister (*Bored*): Hurry, hurry, hurry! That's all you think about. If I don't conserve my energy, how will I be able to dance with the Prince tonight?

Stepmother: But it's almost noon. That leaves only eight hours for you to get ready. By the way, where is your sister? (*She sits down.*)

Stepsister: Up in our room.

Stepmother: Is she dressing?

Stepsister: Not yet.

Stepmother (*Nervously*): Why not? Doesn't she know what time it is?

1st Stepsister: Last week when you saw our room in such a mess, you made the rule that the last one out of bed in the morning had to clean the room and make the bed. Remember?

Stepmother: Yes, I remember.

1st Stepsister: Well, sister is still in bed.

Stepmother: Perhaps the poor dear is tired. After all, a growing girl needs plenty of rest.

1st Stepsister: Yes, but a week of it?

Stepmother: Do you mean it's been a week since she made the bed?

1st Stepsister: No, it's been a week since she got out of bed.

Stepmother: We simply can't have this! It's intolerable indolence, disgraceful lethargy! I'll have Cinderella clean your room and make the bed. She can work it in between milking the cows and washing the clothes. After all, a growing girl needs plenty of exercise. (*Calls*) Cinderella! Cinderella!

Cinderella (*Entering*): Yes, Mother?

STEPMOTHER: Shut the window. I can't stand hearing those birds sing.

CINDERELLA: Of course, Mother.

STEPMOTHER: And stop calling me Mother! It's *Step*-mother — *Step*mother!

CINDERELLA: Yes, *Step*mother. Anything else, *Step*-mother?

STEPMOTHER: Go upstairs, wake up your other step-sister and make her bed. Then help her get ready for the Grand Ball, where her natural beauty and charm will captivate the Prince, and he will marry her and they will live happily ever after! (*Curtain*)

*   *   *   *   *

SCENE 2

SETTING: *Same as Scene 1.*

AT RISE: NARRATOR *enters.*

NARRATOR: There it is: Scene 1 — short, yet long enough to spin the intricate web of intrigue necessary to engage the viewers in various speculations until a satisfying conclusion is reached. Of course, if you've read the story, you already know about all that. Scene 2 also takes place at the Stepmother's house — but later. After eight long hours of brushing hair and teeth, attaching eyelashes and earrings, smear-ing rouge and lipstick, and painting fingernails and toenails — in case they lose a slipper — Cinderella's two stepsisters, and the Stepmother, too, depart for the Grand Ball, where their natural beauty and charm will captivate the Prince, and he will marry them and they will live happily ever after. Now, on with the story! (*He exits right, as* CINDERELLA *enters left.*)

CINDERELLA: I've hurried through my work so fast, I've nothing left to do. (FAIRY GODMOTHER *enters right, brandishing her magic wand.*)

FAIRY GODMOTHER (*Waving wand with flourish*): Presto — chango — alakazam ... and Open Sesame!

CINDERELLA: What? Who are you?

FAIRY GODMOTHER: I am your ... I am here to ... ah-h-h ... I came to ... I was summoned ... ah-h-h ... I ... I ... I don't know.

CINDERELLA (*Pointing to wand*): A wand! I'll bet you're my Fairy Godmother!

FAIRY GODMOTHER: Yes! That's right. I'm your Fairy Godmother. You are Little Red Riding Hood, and I'm here to save you from the Three Little Pigs.

CINDERELLA: No, I'm Cinderella.

FAIRY GODMOTHER (*Puzzled*): Well, what *are* you doing here with the Three Little Pigs?

CINDERELLA: I don't live here with the Three Little Pigs. I live here with my stepmother and two stepsisters. Three ... three, ah-h-h, people.

FAIRY GODMOTHER: What happened to Little Red Riding Hood?

CINDERELLA: I don't know about Little Red Riding Hood. All I know is that I'm supposed to get a gorgeous hairdo, a beautiful new evening gown — with sparkly slippers to match — and a coach and four, to take me to the Grand Ball, where my natural beauty and charm will captivate the Prince, and he will marry me and we'll live happily ever after.

FAIRY GODMOTHER: So that's it. O.K. Let's start with the coach. (*Circles wand in air, pauses*) Is that a basketball or a football coach?

CINDERELLA: No, no! A horse-drawn coach to take me to the Ball.

FAIRY GODMOTHER: Oh, yes. I remember now. Just show me the pumpkin patch, and I'll hocus-pocus it right up.

CINDERELLA: What about my new clothes?

FAIRY GODMOTHER: Of course, first your gown. Let's see now, where is my wand?

CINDERELLA: In your hand.

FAIRY GODMOTHER (*Raising wand and waving it in circle*): Oh, yes! Now ... Bubble, bubble, toil and trouble ... (*Breaking off suddenly*) By the way, what time is it?

CINDERELLA: I don't know. Why?

FAIRY GODMOTHER: Well, I just remembered that you have to be home at twelve o'clock. If you don't know what time it is, how will you know when to leave the ball?

CINDERELLA: I never thought of that.

FAIRY GODMOTHER: Let me try this wand and find out. (*Again flourishes wand*) Bulova, Bulova, toil and Timex. Tell me — (*Knock on door is heard.*)

CINDERELLA: Who could that be? (*Calling*) Come in! (CLOCK *enters quickly with jaunty step, snapping his fingers as he approaches* CINDERELLA.)

CLOCK (*Snapping his fingers to beat of popular dance*

step which he does): A tick and a tock, a tick and a tock ... It's Time, Baby, Time. (*Snaps fingers again and continues with new dance step, and rhythmical "ticking"*) Tick, tock ... tick-tock, tick; tick, tock, tick-tock tick; tick, tock, tick-tock tick.

CINDERELLA: Time? Time for what?

CLOCK: Grand Ball time, chickie-baby. Let's swing! (*Continues dancing, ticking, and finger-snapping.*)

CINDERELLA: With you?

CLOCK: Of course, little lady. Big Mamma here said you needed time and that's my bag. Let's get where it's at! (*Softly*) Tick; tick-tock. Tick-tick-tock. Tick; tick-tock.

CINDERELLA: All right, but this sure isn't the way I thought it would be. (*To* GODMOTHER) What about my clothes?

FAIRY GODMOTHER: Just wait one minute. I'll wave my ... (*Looks at wand in puzzlement*) my ... my ...

CINDERELLA: Wand.

FAIRY GODMOTHER: Yes, that's it — my wand! I'll wave my wand and when I count to three you shall have them. Ready? One — two ... ah-h-h-h ... two (*Pauses*) — ah-h-h ...

CINDERELLA: Three?

FAIRY GODMOTHER (*Jumping joyfully*): Yes — THREE! (*Curtain*)

*   *   *   *   *

SCENE 3

SETTING: *Same as Scenes 1 and 2.*
AT RISE: NARRATOR *enters.*

NARRATOR: Well, the Grand Ball is over and it was a blast. Everything started out as planned. Cinderella arrived in a gorgeous hairdo, a beautiful new evening gown, with sparkly slippers to match, and all her natural beauty and charm would have captivated the Prince right then and there, if some nutty clock had not jumped up and yelled, "Time for the Sock-hop!" So-o-o, all the shoes were kicked into a big pile in the middle of the floor, and the whole crowd danced till curfew. And now we are ready for the final and summarizing scene, where we should learn the answer to the question: How will the Prince ever find the right slipper for the right foot, so he can get married and live happily ever after? Let us begin at the end. (NARRATOR *exits, as* TWO STEPSISTERS *enter right. They plod across stage to chairs, plop themselves down, resting heads on hands, yawning, then shifting to rest heads on other hand, yawning from time to time.* 2ND STEPSISTER *dozes off.*)

1ST STEPSISTER (*Calling loudly*): Cinderella! Cinderella! (CINDERELLA *enters promptly.*)

CINDERELLA: Yes, Stepsister?

1ST STEPSISTER: Shut the window. Those birds are driving me batty.

CINDERELLA: It would be a pleasure, Stepsister. (*Shuts window, then exits.* 1ST STEPSISTER *falls asleep, and* 2ND STEPSISTER *wakes with a start.*)

2ND STEPSISTER: Cinderella! Cinderella! (CINDERELLA *runs in.*)

CINDERELLA: You called, Stepsister?

2ND STEPSISTER: Can't you regulate that stupid window?

CINDERELLA: I'll try, Stepsister. (*Opens window and continues to stand by it, opening and closing it as directed by motions from* 2ND STEPSISTER.)

STEPMOTHER (*Entering*): Land sakes, girls! Why aren't you getting your feet ready to fit into the slipper, so your natural beauty and charm will —

2ND STEPSISTER: Come off it, Mother! You know I'll never get these size nines into those little slippers. (*Irritably*) Cinderella, close that window!

CINDERELLA: Of course, Stepsister — anything to please! (*She bangs down window, and* 1ST STEPSISTER *wakes with a start.*)

STEPMOTHER (*To* 1ST STEPSISTER): Well, it's about time you woke up. We have plans to make so that you can get ready to fit into the slipper, so your natural beauty ...

1ST STEPSISTER: Maybe lying in bed for the next week, resting, would help shrink my feet. (*There is a loud knocking at the door.*)

STEPMOTHER: Cinderella, open the door. (CINDERELLA *scurries to open door, and* PRINCE *enters, followed by* COURTIER, *and* PAGE, *who has large box of shoes on large pillow.* COURTIER *holds scroll from which he reads.*)

COURTIER (*Reading*): Hear ye, hear ye! It is hereby commanded by Royal Edict that every woman who was in attendance at the Grand Ball shall have the opportunity to try on these shoes to determine who will be worthy of joining the Prince of the Realm —

STEPMOTHER: Yes! Yes! We know all that. Let's get on with the fitting! (*She rushes to box* PAGE *is carrying, grabs pair of shoes and runs to give them to* 1ST

STEPSISTER, *then runs back, grabs another pair and gives them to* 2ND STEPSISTER.) Now hurry, girls. See if the shoes fit. (*They put shoes on quickly.*)

1ST STEPSISTER (*Holding out her feet with shoes on*): These fit perfectly.

2ND STEPSISTER: So do these.

CINDERELLA: But, Prince, does this mean that you are going to marry *both* of them?

PRINCE: Who said anything about marrying them? After the Ball I was left with a mountain of used shoes. I'm recruiting an army of sales clerks to open a whole new chain of shoe stores. (*To* COURTIER, *pointing to* STEPSISTERS) These two will do!

STEPMOTHER: But what about living happily . . .

PRINCE (*Breaking in and pointing to* STEPMOTHER): You can take her along, too.

COURTIER: All right, now. Attention! Forward, march. Hut, two, three, four! Hut, two, three, four! Hut, two . . . (COURTIER *continues counting as he marches* STEPSISTERS *and* STEPMOTHER *offstage.*)

PRINCE (*Arms outstretched to* CINDERELLA): And now, at last, I have time for you!

CLOCK (*Rushing in*): *Time!* Did you say *Time?* Well, wind me up and ring my chime! (*Snapping fingers, he begins rhythmic dance.*) Tick, tock, tick-tock tick. Tick, tock, tick-tock tick. And a tick, tock . . .

PRINCE (*Embracing* CINDERELLA): Our love shall be timeless.

CINDERELLA (*Turning to the audience*): This has got to be the end! (*Quick curtain*)

THE END

The Way-Out Wizard of Oz

Whatever happened to the Yellow Brick Road?

Characters

DOROTHY, *who wants to go back to Kansas*
WIZARD OF OZ, *who has a broken wand*
SCARECROW, *who wants to be good-looking*
PLASTICMAN, *who needs a battery power cell*
LIONESS, *who likes to compete and wants medals to show for it*
WICKED WITCH OF THE NORTH, *the same mean, old one*

SETTING: *Forest, with backdrop of sky, clouds, bushes, and exotic trees, in unusual colors and shapes.*
AT RISE: SCARECROW *is leaning against crossed boards, left, as if hanging. There are a few cornstalks around him.* PLASTICMAN *is hidden behind bushes, right.*

DOROTHY (*Entering as if blown by storm, tumbling and rolling on floor, coming to a stop in sitting position down center*): Ooooh-h-h-h-h-h! Help! Where am I? (*Gets up and looks around*) Oh, now I know.

64

We had this terrible storm in Kansas and I've been blown to the land of Oz. Oh, Aunt Em! Aunt Em! I want to come home! (*Starts to sob, then stops*) Wait, that won't help! I might as well get on with the Yellow Brick Road, "Over the Rainbow," and the silver shoes that protect me from the Wicked Witch of the North. Let's see ... first the silver shoes. (*Looking around*) Where could they be? (*Moves up left with back to audience.* WIZARD OF OZ *enters right, looking all around, as if lost and trying to determine where he is. He moves down center while* DOROTHY *moves up and opposite, looking away from* WIZARD *toward scenery. They continue in a circular motion, not noticing each other, until they bump, back to back, in center stage.*)

WIZARD OF OZ: Oh! Hello! Who are you?

DOROTHY: I'm Dorothy, from Kansas. I'm looking for the silver shoes so I can walk up the Yellow Brick Road and sing "Over the Rainbow."

WIZARD: Hold it! Ho-o-ol-l-ld it! Silver shoes? Yellow Brick Road? "Over the Rainbow"? Where did you say you were from?

DOROTHY: Kansas, and I want to find the Wonderful Wizard of Oz so he can help me get back to Kansas!

WIZARD: The Wizard of Oz? Why didn't you say so? I'd like to find Oz myself.

DOROTHY: You would? Oh! You must be the Scarecrow. You're looking for a brain!

WIZARD: No, I —

DOROTHY: The Tinman — looking for a heart?

WIZARD: No, you see, I —

DOROTHY: You're certainly no lion!

WIZARD: That's true. Actually, you see, I'm the Wizard.

DOROTHY: What?

WIZARD: The Wizard ... the Wonderful Wizard of Oz.

DOROTHY: Then why do you want to come with me to find you if you aren't there, but here?

WIZARD OF OZ: I'd like to go with you *not* to *find* me, but to find where I should be if I were not here with you looking for me. Understand?

DOROTHY: I think so. What it means is ...

WIZARD: I'm lost.

DOROTHY: Why don't you just wave your wand and "magic" yourself back to Oz?

WIZARD (*Showing broken wand*): Because my wand is broken, and a broken wand is no better than ... than a ... a ...

DOROTHY: A broken teacup?

WIZARD: Right! It just won't work.

DOROTHY: Then where does that leave me? How will I get back to Kansas?

WIZARD: You go right ahead and follow the Yellow Brick Road and look for me — ah, that is, look for where I would be if I were not here with you looking for me. When you do find where I should be, I'll be home, and I can repair my wand.

DOROTHY: Then you'll send me back to Kansas?

WIZARD: I can't make any promises. I already have a broken wand. I don't want a broken promise, too.

DOROTHY: O.K., but first — if I remember correctly

— I have to find those silver shoes. (*Looks all around*)

WIZARD (*Sitting downstage, dejectedly examining broken wand*): Silver shoes? Haven't seen them. Sure wish I could be a bigger help.

SOUND: *Sound of chimes is heard. Silver shoes appear onstage.* (*See Production Notes.*)

DOROTHY (*Noticing "magic" appearance of shoes*): What was that? Look! The silver shoes! You said you wished you could help me and "ding" (*Imitates chimes*), they just appeared! (*She picks up shoes and puts them on.* WIZARD *remains seated, paying no attention to what has just happened.*)

WIZARD: Oh, no, that was no magic. The shoes were there all along. I could never make magic with a broken wand. A broken wand is no better than a . . . a . . .

DOROTHY: A broken fence back in Kansas?

WIZARD: Right! It just won't work.

DOROTHY (*Standing*): Wow! These shoes fit perfectly! Now, on to the Yellow Brick Road! (*Looks both ways*) I wonder where it is?

SCARECROW (*Pointing first one arm, then the other, in floppy manner*): I would say go that way, and then back that way.

DOROTHY (*Huddling close to* WIZARD): Who said that? (*Looks at* SCARECROW) Of course! You're the Scarecrow and you're looking for a brain. (*She helps "unhook"* SCARECROW *from pole.*)

SCARECROW (*Stretching and shaking arms and legs*): Brain? Why would anyone want a brain? Nobody uses brains today. A long time ago a few people used them — in business and politics — but no more. What a guy needs today is good looks: white teeth, manageable hair, a clean, fresh smell. No-o-o-o, no brain for me. What I want is good looks.

DOROTHY: You're supposed to get a diploma to show that you have a brain. But, now that I think about it, I do know a lot of people who have diplomas and no brains.

SCARECROW: Another thing. Did you ever see a brain win a popularity contest? No! Never! Good looks, that's what wins!

DOROTHY: Then what you need from the Wizard is a grooming kit. Something with a mirror, comb, toothbrush, nail file — all those things to keep you well groomed. Isn't that right, Wizard?

WIZARD: That sounds very logical. (*Examining broken wand*) I just wish I could help you get it.

SOUND: *Chimes are heard and kit appears.*

DOROTHY: Look! There it is! (*She gives kit to* SCARE-CROW, *who takes mirror out and starts primping.*)

WIZARD: Say, little lady, you're pretty good at finding things! When we get back to Oz maybe you could look for my favorite golf shirt. I haven't been able to find it for weeks.

DOROTHY: But *I'm* not finding things. It's you and your wand!

WIZARD: My wand? Oh, no! My wand is broken. And a broken wand is no better than a ... no better than a ...

SCARECROW: A broken stalk in a cornfield?

WIZARD: Right! It just doesn't work.

DOROTHY: If you say so. I suppose we'd better go on to the Yellow Brick —

PLASTICMAN (*Behind bushes; making growling sounds*): Er-er-er-er-er-er . . . .

DOROTHY: Did you hear something?

SCARECROW: Just a minute ago I heard "ding." (*Imitates chimes*)

DOROTHY: No! No! I mean just now. Something like —

PLASTICMAN (*Behind bushes*): Er-er-er-er . . . .

DOROTHY: See, there it is again! (*Moves to bushes and pushes them aside, revealing* PLASTICMAN) Hey, look! It's the Tinman! (SCARECROW *and* WIZARD *join her.*)

PLASTICMAN (*Speaking without moving*): No-no-no-no-no . . . .

DOROTHY: I'll bet he needs oil.

SCARECROW: No. (*Reading directions printed on* PLASTICMAN) The directions say, "To operate, place key in slot and wind counterclockwise."

DOROTHY: O.K. (*Looking*) But where's the key?

SCARECROW: I don't see one, but wait! I think my new nail file will fit in there. (*Moves to back of* PLASTICMAN, *simulates winding with file. Offstage winding noise is heard.*)

PLASTICMAN (*Beginning to move arms, then fingers, then head, legs, etc.*): Yes, yes! That's it! Keep winding! Oh! Ah-h-h! Ooooooo! This is the first time I have stretched in ages!

DOROTHY: What happened, Mr. Tinman?

PLASTICMAN: First of all, let's clear up a few things.

I'm *not* a *tin* man. Tin went out with hula hoops and five-cent candy bars. I'm made from tough, durable plastic. I never rust, corrode, or break. My problem is that somebody's always losing my key. (*To* SCARECROW) That was really smart thinking on your part to use that nail file.

SCARECROW: Aw-w-w! It wasn't smart, just the result of good grooming.

DOROTHY: What you need from the Wizard is a new wind-up key.

PLASTICMAN: Oh, no! I've had it with that "wind-up-lose-the-key" jazz. What I want is to be converted to a rechargeable, electric power cell — AC and/or DC — something I can plug in at night that will never run down during the day.

DOROTHY: Yes! Of course! A rechargeable battery! That wouldn't be too hard to get, would it, Wizard?

WIZARD: Oh, that would be easy for a Wizard with a good wand. But mine is broken — see? — and like this it's no better than a broken ... a broken....

PLASTICMAN: A broken electrical circuit?

WIZARD: Right! It just won't work. But a power cell is a great idea. I sure wish I could help you get one. (*He continues to study wand.*)

SOUND: *Chimes are heard and electric cell appears. (Cardboard box with several wires, resembling over-sized battery, can be used.)*

DOROTHY: There you are, Mr. Plasticman, power to spare. (*She and* SCARECROW *simulate wiring cell into* PLASTICMAN.)

PLASTICMAN: What happened? How did you find that?

WIZARD: That girl could find five Tuesdays in a month of Sundays.

DOROTHY: I must be getting help from someone. Let's just say it's magic. (*Points at* WIZARD, *who is examining wand, and puts finger to lips warningly. Others nod in acknowledgment.* WIZARD *still does not know he is causing "magic."*)

LIONESS (*Entering in a rush*): R-r-rooaaar-r-r! (*Spits and paws, snarling, at group, who cower behind* DOROTHY.)

DOROTHY: Hold it, everybody! Don't be afraid of this lion. He's really just a coward.

PLASTICMAN: Oh, is that a lion? (*Steps out in front of group*) A lion can't hurt me. I'm made of tough, durable plastic. I won't rust, corrode, or be chewed up. Down, Mr. Lion! Down!

LIONESS: Lion? *MISTER* Lion? (*Blows whistle*) Time out! Five-yard penalty! Strike one! Do you see a long, shaggy mane?

PLASTICMAN: No, but —

LIONESS: Strike two! Do you see a dirty-dapple-tan color?

PLASTICMAN: Well, I —

LIONESS: Strike three! Now get this, misinformed persons, that makes me a lioness, not a lion! Three strikes, you're out. I win!

DOROTHY: We're out? You win? What are we playing?

LIONESS: We're playing Equal Athletic Competition for Women. (*Looks at* DOROTHY's *shoes*) Hey, I think your silver shoes are a real winner. Want to race me for 50 meters?

DOROTHY: No, what I want is to go back to Kansas.

LIONESS: Kansas! With those silver shoes I thought sure you were Josephine Namath of pro football fame.

DOROTHY: No, I'm Dorothy. What happened to the lion, the King of Beasts?

LIONESS: *"King"* of Beasts? *"King"* of Beasts! Why should the "King" job only be open to men? Women can compete, too. With shoes like that you've just got to be a sport. Tennis? (*To others*) Anyone?

DOROTHY: Thank you, no. I just want to get home to Kansas. But I do agree with you that women should be able to compete with men and get the same rewards. That's only fair.

WICKED WITCH (*Entering*): Heh, heh, heh! Fair, is it? Too bad you'll never have a chance to find out. You know what I want, so hurry up and hand them over!

DOROTHY: Oh, no! It's the Wicked Witch of the North and she's here to take my silver shoes! Wizard, what shall I do?

WIZARD (*Cowering with* SCARECROW *behind* DOROTHY): Don't count on me! You know I can't do anything with a broken wand. A broken wand like this is no better than a . . . than a . . . .

LIONESS: A broken play in a football game?

WIZARD: Right! It just doesn't work!

PLASTICMAN: I'll protect all of you. I'm made of tough, durable plastic that won't rust, corrode or break.

WICKED WITCH: Heh, heh, heh. But can you resist my magic spells?

PLASTICMAN (*Standing resolutely in front of group,*

with arms crossed): I'm willing to find out — are you?

WICKED WITCH: Isn't this touching. A broken wand and a bottle of bleach trying to stand between me and what I want. You know those silver shoes are mine, and I intend to get them no matter what I have to do!

LIONESS (*Blowing whistle*): Time out! Before we continue this game, I think we need to review the rules.

WICKED WITCH: Stay out of this, you overgrown pussycat, or I'll call in a tiger to tame you.

LIONESS: Oh-oh! (*Blows whistle*) Foul! You are penalized five yards for intimidation.

WICKED WITCH: Oh, yeah? And just who is going to step it off?

LIONESS (*Moving toward* WITCH, *spitting, snarling, and clawing in cat-like manner*): This will be more fun than beating Bobby Riggs.

WICKED WITCH (*Backing slowly*): Now, now, wait a minute. Hold on! (*Backs faster*) Let's talk this over! (*Exits*) Help!

LIONESS: There, game's over. I win!

DOROTHY: Yes, and you were great! You deserve a gold medal! Right, Wizard?

WIZARD: That's true. In fact, for such an outstanding victory as that, you should have the game trophy for the most valuable player, too. I just wish I could get them for you.

SOUND: *Chimes ring. Medal and trophy appear.* DOROTHY *pins medal on* LIONESS*'s chest,* PLASTIC-MAN *hands her trophy, and* SCARECROW *shakes her* *hand.* WIZARD *continues to study wand, dejected.*

WIZARD: But what can I do? My wand is broken. Everybody knows a broken wand is no better than a ... no better than a ... whatever. But one thing is certain: when we do get back to Oz I want to place all of you on my staff. (*To* SCARECROW) A clever, good-looking guy like you should head my public relations team.

SCARECROW: I owe it all to the results of good grooming.

WIZARD (*To* PLASTICMAN): And the way you stayed in there when the Wicked Witch of the North threatened to use magic shows that you will never run down. I want you to be the Captain of my Castle Guard.

PLASTICMAN: It's only because I have a rechargeable power cell.

WIZARD (*To* LIONESS): And I would like you to organize athletic competition for the youth of Oz.

LIONESS: For both boys *and girls?*

WIZARD: Of course — with medals and trophies awarded equally to all.

SCARECROW: We could call it the *O*zlympic Games.

WIZARD: Great idea!

PLASTICMAN: What about Dorothy? (*Nudges* LIONESS, *knowing they can get* WIZARD *to use "magic"*)

LIONESS: Yes, what about Dorothy? She wants to go home. (*Nudges* SCARECROW *to continue*)

SCARECROW: I sure wish we could help her get back to Kansas.

WIZARD: Yes, me, too.

SOUND: *Chimes are heard and airline flight bag with a ticket tied to handle appears.*

DOROTHY: Look at this! A non-stop 747 Boeing Balloon to Kansas, leaving (*Looking at watch*) now! (*Looks offstage*) There it is! Goodbye, everybody! (*Exits*)

SCARECROW (*Watching offstage*): She's going home to Kansas.

PLASTICMAN: There she goes — over the rainbow!

LIONESS: I sure did like her shoes!

WIZARD: I knew she'd find a way home. That girl could find anything. I sure wish we could find Oz.

SOUND: *Chimes ring. (Quick curtain.)*

THE END

PTA Triumphs Again

A mini-melodrama

Characters

ANNOUNCER
PTA MOM
ARCH VILLAIN
DARLING NELL
HERO
TWO SIGN HOLDERS

SCENE 1

BEFORE RISE: ANNOUNCER *enters in front of curtain.*
ANNOUNCER: We now present for your histrionic pleasure the moving melodrama, *PTA Triumphs Again!* Our players include the lovable, harried PTA Mom. (PTA MOM *enters and crosses to front of stage, as pianist in orchestra pit plays "Home, Sweet Home," or other appropriate melody.*) She is honored in her community for being a Little League Umpire, a Girl Scout Leader, and a prize-winning apple pie baker! (MOM *smiles modestly.*) But, more important, as

the proud mother of two girls and two boys, she is a dedicated member of the Abraham Lincoln Elementary School PTA, the Teddy Roosevelt Junior High PTA, the George Washington Senior High PTA, and, now that her oldest daughter is starting college, she is founding the first chapter of State University PTA! (TWO SIGN HOLDERS *enter right and left with signs reading* APPLAUSE *and* HOORAY! *They applaud and cheer to encourage audience, then exit with* PTA MOM.) Another member of the cast is the mean and vile Arch Villain. (ARCH VILLAIN *enters to sinister music, wrapping his cape around him. He slithers to center, twirling moustache and emitting menacing laugh.* SIGN HOLDERS *re-enter with signs reading* HISS *and* BOO. *They lead audience in hissing and booing* VILLAIN, *then exit.* VILLAIN *remains onstage, stalking about.*) Unfortunately, we will see all too much of this wretched miscreant. (VILLAIN *shakes fist at* ANNOUNCER, *then exits with evil laugh, as* SIGN HOLDERS *re-enter with* HISS *and* BOO *signs.*) The next member of the cast is one we can never see enough of — our heroine, the lovely and innocent Darling Nell, PTA Mom's oldest daughter. (DARLING NELL *enters to "Spring Song," or other appropriate music, and trips innocently to center, fluttering her lashes.* SIGN HOLDERS *flip signs to read* APPLAUSE *and* HOORAY! NELL *curtsies, then turns to exit just as* ARCH VILLAIN *re-enters, laughing and twirling moustache.* DARLING NELL *puts back of hand to brow, recoils, then exits with* VILLAIN *in pursuit.* SIGN HOLDERS *flip signs to read*

HISS *and* BOO.) Last, but certainly not least, is the noble Hero! (HERO *rushes in and flexes muscles, as appropriate music plays.* SIGN HOLDERS *flip signs to read* APPLAUSE *and* HOORAY!, *then exit quickly with* HERO.) Now that you have met the players, let us proceed with the agonizing yet inspiring melodrama, *PTA Triumphs Again.* (*Exits.* SIGN HOLDERS *re-enter with* APPLAUSE *and* HOORAY! *signs, lead audience in cheering for* ANNOUNCER, *then exit. Curtain rises.*)

SETTING: *PTA Mom's living room, decorated with old-fashioned furnishings, including rocking chair, family photographs, floor lamps, and large sampler reading* GOD BLESS THE PTA.

AT RISE: PTA MOM *enters with happy smile, as pianist plays appropriate music. She sits down in rocker and picks up knitting.*

PTA MOM: Oh, what a fun day this has been! This morning we had a breakfast for Honorary Life Members of the PTA, then at ten o'clock a PTA Board Meeting at the senior high, a "bring-your-own-salad" luncheon at the junior high at noon, then this afternoon I baked cookies for the regular elementary PTA meeting tonight. (*Loud, ominous knock is heard from offstage.* MOM *calls sweetly.*) Please enter. I welcome the world into my home. (VILLAIN *enters menacingly. Sinister music plays.* SIGN HOLDERS *enter left and right with* HISS *and* BOO *signs, then exit.*)

VILLAIN (*Chuckling*): It is October, my fine widow,

and I have come for the payment on your 1958 Chevrolet station wagon — with radio, heater, and whitewall tires.

PTA MOM: Oh, gracious me! It cannot be October already! School has just begun!

VILLAIN: But it is October! (*Chuckles evilly*) It is time for the payment. (SIGN HOLDERS *enter with* HISS *and* BOO *signs, then exit.*)

PTA MOM: But, merciful heavens! I don't have the money! There were book fees, tuition fees, enrollment fees, medical fees, dental fees, Little League fees, PTA fees . . . our free public education is costing me a fortune!

VILLAIN (*Holding hands over ears and looking away*): I shall not hear excuses — you *must* make the payment!

PTA MOM: But I can't make the payment!

VILLAIN: Then I must take away your 1958 Chevrolet station wagon — with radio, heater, and whitewall tires!

PTA MOM: Oh, worry and suffering! You cannot do this to me! How will I ever get to the PTA meetings?

VILLAIN: Then you must make the payment.

PTA MOM: But I cannot. Oh, shame and humility! I have never missed a payment in all my five years of ownership — and this was the last installment! Can't you wait just a few days?

VILLAIN (*Shaking head*): Our policy is "no pay — no way."

PTA MOM: But I simply cannot pay! (*Wrings her hands*) Alas and alack! Whatever shall I do?

VILLAIN (*Twirling moustache and laughing evilly*): If you cannot pay, there is *another* way. (*Rubs his hands together eagerly*)

PTA MOM: Great gratification! Another way! Tell me, tell me!

VILLAIN: If you cannot pay, and do not want me to take the car, then you must let your daughter, Darling Nell, marry me! (*Laughs as sinister music plays.* SIGN HOLDERS *re-enter with* BOO *and* HISS *signs, then exit.*)

PTA MOM: No, no, no! (*Puts back of hand to forehead*) This cannot be! She loves another!

VILLAIN: Then I must take the car.

PTA MOM: But I need the car! Oh, agony and torment!

VILLAIN: There are only two choices: Your car, or your daughter. You have until six o'clock to decide! (*Laughs. Sinister music plays.* SIGN HOLDERS *enter with* HISS *and* BOO *signs.* VILLAIN *exits.* MOM *wrings her hands as curtain closes.*)

*　　*　　*　　*　　*

SCENE 2

BEFORE RISE: ANNOUNCER *enters.*

ANNOUNCER: Before we return to the gripping climax of our play, let us take a moment for each and every one of you to consider the mental agony and torment that this conscientious example of American motherhood and Honorary Life Member of the PTA must now be suffering. What will she do? What *can* she do? If she keeps her station wagon, Darling Nell must marry the Villain! Yet if she loses her car, how can she get to the PTA? The suspense is unbearable! Let us conclude with the conclusion, and discover whether PTA Mom will choose alternative number one, or number two. (*Exits. Curtain rises.*)

SETTING: *Same as Scene 1.*

AT RISE: PTA MOM *is sitting in rocking chair, dabbing at her eyes with handkerchief. Sad music is played.*

PTA MOM: Oh woe is me, woe is me! (DARLING NELL *enters, smiling.*)

DARLING NELL: Mother, you seem distressed! Whatever can the trouble be? (*Bats eyes*)

PTA MOM: Oh dreadful dilemma! I have an impossible decision to make and only a very short time in which to render it.

DARLING NELL: Tell me, Mother. Perhaps I, in the sweet innocence of youth (*Flutters eyelids at audience*), can help you.

PTA MOM: No, no. Since the resulting consequences could affect your future, the decision must remain with me to make.

DARLING NELL: But Mother, I want to help you.

PTA MOM: Nay, sweet child, I alone must decide. Pray tell me, what do you think of Arch Villain?

DARLING NELL (*Staggering back*): Oh, Mother, I loathe and despise the insufferable, repulsive knave!

(SIGN HOLDERS *enter with* APPLAUSE *and* HOORAY *signs.*)

PTA MOM: I mean as a husband.

DARLING NELL: No! No! I could never marry the treacherous cad.

PTA MOM: Well (*Sighs*), I guess I should prepare for some long walks. (ARCH VILLAIN *knocks and enters. Sinister music plays.* SIGN HOLDERS *show* HISS *and* BOO *signs.*)

VILLAIN (*To* MOM): It is six o'clock. The time has arrived. Are you prepared for me to marry your oldest daughter, Darling Nell?

DARLING NELL (*Backing away*): No, no — a hundred times no! (SIGN HOLDERS *show* APPLAUSE *and* HOORAY *signs.*)

VILLAIN (*To* PTA MOM): Madam, your daughter rebuffs my act of charity and good will! Very well, if that is your decision, I shall take the 1958 Chevrolet station wagon — with radio, heater, and whitewall tires! (*Holds out hand*) The keys, please!

PTA MOM: No, no! A thousand times no!

VILLAIN: Aha! Then what is your decision? (*Advances on* DARLING NELL, *who squeals.*)

PTA MOM (*Lifting hands helplessly*): Oh, doom and despair! What choice do I have? (*There is a knock offstage and* HERO *rushes in. Triumphant music plays. He smiles and flexes muscles.*)

HERO: Dry your eyes and fear no more, my lady. I shall remedy the situation!

PTA MOM: Why? Are you the Hero?

HERO: Yes! I will make the final payment on your 1958

station wagon — with radio, heater, and whitewall tires — and, I am also the man who has promised to wcd your lovely daughter, Darling Nell.

DARLING NELL (*Stepping next to him, fluttering eyes, and holding hands to heart*): My hero! (SIGN HOLDERS *show* APPLAUSE *and* HOORAY *signs.*)

PTA MOM: But just who are you?

HERO: Don't you recognize me? I am the principal of the school!

VILLAIN: A principal? A principal? Ha! Just how do you propose to get a car payment amounting to one hundred and forty-five dollars and fifty-seven cents?

PTA MOM: Oh, great pity and sorrow! Then you *can't* make the payment?

HERO: But I *can* make the payment! You have been such a dedicated member of the PTA that they decided to raise the money!

PTA MOM: Virtue and justice triumph again!

VILLAIN: Curses! Foiled again by the PTA! (*Triumphant music plays.* SIGN HOLDERS *lead audience in cheering as* MOM, HERO *and* NELL *form a tableau at center, and* VILLAIN *slinks off. Curtain.*)

THE END

Pinocchio in Equal Opportunity Land

A modern turnabout

Characters

NARRATOR
PINOCCHIO
GEPPETTO
FAIRY MODMOTHER
SHIRLEY TEMPLE
CUSTOMER

SCENE 1

BEFORE RISE: NARRATOR *enters in front of curtain.*
NARRATOR: The story you are about to see is true. It's
about the marionette, Pinocchio, and how he came
to be a real, live boy. We had to change the plot,
shift the time, alter the theme, shuffle the setting,
vary the scene, convert the characters, and modify
the costumes — but *all* the rest is absolutely *true.*
You may remember the old story. Geppetto the Toy-
maker wants a son, so he handcrafts this wooden
kid. Well, the kid's a real brat who gets into all kinds

of trouble, until the end of the story, when he finally turns out to be A-O.K. That's the ancient version. Today the story would be more like this . . . (*Exits as curtains open*)

SETTING: *Geppetto's toy shop, cluttered with wagons, drums, dolls, hobby-horses, toy soldiers, etc. There is a workbench downstage.*

AT RISE: GEPPETTO *is at workbench attaching final string to leg of marionette,* PINOCCHIO, *who is propped up on workbench.* SHIRLEY TEMPLE, *as a doll, is leaning against leg of workbench. Both are motionless until cued.*

GEPPETTO: There, all finished! Now, what shall I call you? (*Pauses*) How about Pinocchio? (*Uses his hand to move* PINOCCHIO's *head up and down*) Oh, you like the name! How do you like my toy shop? (*Moves* PINOCCHIO's *head from side to side, then up and down again*) Well, I like it too. And, I like you. In fact, what I would like most of all would be to have a real, live boy just like you.

FAIRY MODMOTHER (*Entering quickly as though by magic*): Shazam, flimflam, and alakazam! Hang in there, Old One, your very own, personal, genuine, Fairy Modmother is — presto! — at your service. (*Does popular dance step around room*)

GEPPETTO: Wonderful! A fairy godmother — just like in the story books!

MODMOTHER: Not a fairy godmother, man — Fairy Modmother! And in *no* way am I "just like in the story books"!

GEPPETTO: If this is not like the story books, how did you know I needed you?

MODMOTHER: Get serious! It's a Fairy Modmother's bag to know all — see all — hear all!

GEPPETTO: Then it *is* like the story books! You've come to turn this piece of painted wood (*Indicates* PINOCCHIO) into a real, live boy. Oh, I can hardly wait!

MODMOTHER: Cool it. I'm here to make with the magic, all right, but there's no way we can do it like the story books.

GEPPETTO: You mean Pinocchio will not tell fibs? (MODMOTHER *shakes head as each question is asked*) Not grow a long nose? No donkey ears? No man-eating whale?

MODMOTHER: No way!

GEPPETTO: Don't tell me it will be *worse* than that! (*To audience*) What's happening to the youth of today?

MODMOTHER: Nothing more than what already happened to your generation, so don't get all uptight! Now, listen: under today's equal opportunity laws, you have to give girls a fair chance.

GEPPETTO: Girls?

MODMOTHER: Right on!

GEPPETTO: But I want a little boy, not a little girl!

MODMOTHER (*Holding hands over ears*): Oh-h-h-h-h-h! I'm receiving vibes that say, "One Male Chauvinist Lives Here!"

GEPPETTO: But a girl will be nothing but a little woman. She'll say, "This place is a mess!" and want it cleaned up! She'll say, "The workbench is in the wrong place!'' and make me move it over there! (*Points*) And she'll say, "Look at your shirt! You've spilled glue all over it!"

MODMOTHER: Hold it — like hoooolllldddd it! I'm your very own, personal, genuine Fairy Modmother. It's not my bag to cop out on your wishes. What you want is what you get.

GEPPETTO: You mean I get a real, live boy, after all?

MODMOTHER: I mean you will get a *choice*.

GEPPETTO: A choice? You mean you're going to give me both a boy *and* a girl?

MODMOTHER: Now you read me! Then in one week I'll shazam back and put the final zap on the one you want to be real for keeps. (*Turns to* PINOCCHIO) First the boy. (*Points wand at* PINOCCHIO. *Bell sounds offstage.*)

PINOCCHIO (*Coming to life*): Hey, I'm alive! I can jump! (*Hops off workbench*) I can run! (*Skips to front of stage*) I can talk, and yell! (*Shouts*)

MODMOTHER: Now, cool it, kid. Before you jump and run all around the place, you —

PINOCCHIO (*Stopping to look at* MODMOTHER): Daddy! (*Holds out arms to her*)

MODMOTHER: No way! (*To* GEPPETTO) Already I can see that his wooden head will give you problems!

PINOCCHIO: Problems? Not me! I just want to get on with the story: You know, find Little Bo Peep, who will save me from the wicked Queen, who says, "Mirror, mirror on the wall, Humpty Dumpty had a fall."

MODMOTHER: Oh, brother, have you got hang-ups! Sit

up here and let's rap about your assignment. (PINOC-CHIO *climbs onto workbench*) You're Pinocchio.

PINOCCHIO: Pinocchio?

MODMOTHER: Old Geppetto wanted a real, live boy, so we created you.

PINOCCHIO: Created me?

MODMOTHER: Yeah! We made you so that Geppetto won't be lonely.

GEPPETTO: Pinocchio, don't you remember? You've been through the story many times. You come to life, tell fibs, your nose grows, and we get swallowed by a whale.

PINOCCHIO (*Nodding*): Oh, yes! I remember it all now. (*Puzzled*) Who am I? What did I do?

MODMOTHER: Forget all that. Just remember that you're Pinocchio, a boy, and all you have to do in this story is compete with a girl.

PINOCCHIO: Compete?

MODMOTHER: Yeah, *competition,* the American way! Give girls equal opportunity and they can stand up to boys any day!

PINOCCHIO (*Aside to audience*): I don't understand what's going on, and already I don't like it.

GEPPETTO: Pinocchio, what the Fairy Modmother means is this: She's going to give me a boy *and* a girl. After one week of having you both here, I'm to decide which one I want to be made into a real, live — ah, person.

PINOCCHIO: But I don't like girls!

MODMOTHER: No wonder we have prejudice. Two

minutes under Geppetto's roof and already you're a male chauvinist!

PINOCCHIO: And I don't want to compete. Can't we just go back to the old story — telling fibs, growing a long nose?

MODMOTHER: No way! (*Looks around*) Now to zap up a girl. (*Points to* SHIRLEY) How about that one?

GEPPETTO: Great! That's a sweet Shirley Temple doll. I always liked the song (*Singing*) "On the Good Ship Lollypop."

MODMOTHER (*Shrugging*): You want Shirley Temple, you get Shirley Temple. (*Points wand. Bell sounds.*) I've got to go. See you in a week! (*Exits*)

SHIRLEY (*Sweet and sugary*): Hello. (*To* GEPPETTO) You must be my new daddy. I like you. Now, why don't you sit down here and chat with my new brother, Pinocchio, while I go fix supper. O.K.?

GEPPETTO: Well, hello ... and yes, thank you. (*To* PINOCCHIO) I can't imagine why I didn't want a girl!

PINOCCHIO: If this is competition, I think I stand a better chance with the whale! (*Curtain*)

*   *   *   *   *

SCENE 2

BEFORE RISE: NARRATOR *enters in front of curtain.*

NARRATOR: In one moment Scene Two will begin and you, the amazed and fascinated viewing audience, will be caught up once again in the exciting biographical narration. You will learn whom Geppetto will choose as his own real, live — ah, person. But first, the basic points of Scene One should be reiterated to whet your cognitive prowess and ignite your whimsical fantasy: One, Geppetto wanted a boy; two, the Fairy Modmother said a girl must be given an equal opportunity; three, Geppetto had one week to decide which one would be his own real, live — ah, person; and four, now the week has passed and Geppetto must make up his mind. Let Scene Two begin! (*Exits*)

SETTING: *Same as Scene 1.*

AT RISE: GEPPETTO *is working on a toy at cluttered workbench.*

GEPPETTO: There, that's finished. (*Sets toy aside*) Now to work on —

CUSTOMER (*Entering*): Geppetto, congratulate me! I just became a grandfather today!

GEPPETTO: Well, congratulations! (*Shakes* CUSTOMER's *hand*) What was it — a boy, or a girl?

CUSTOMER: A little girl. I want to buy a present for her. I must have a doll like the one that stands in front of your shop every afternoon saying, "Hello. Beautiful day!"

GEPPETTO: The one that dances and sings (*Singing*) "On the Good Ship Lollypop"?

CUSTOMER: Yes, that's the one. That's great advertising! How did you ever happen to think of it?

GEPPETTO: Well, you might say I just — zapped it up.

But you'll have to wait for a doll just like that. I've had so many orders for that Shirley Temple doll this past week that I'm way behind production, and ... (*Reflects*) Did I say week? Has it been a week already?

CUSTOMER: Why, yes! That doll has been there every night for a week. Put me down for one. I want my new granddaughter to have one as soon as possible. (*Crosses to exit*) I'll get it when it's ready. (*Exits*)

GEPPETTO (*Waving; preoccupied*): Oh, my goodness! The Fairy Modmother gave me a week to decide which one and the week has passed already! I have to make up my mind! Which one? Shirley is bright, sweet, considerate, helpful, and has more than doubled my sales. And Pinocchio is ... (PINOCCHIO *enters, wipes nose on shirt sleeve and flops down into chair.*)

PINOCCHIO: Hi, Grandpa Geppetto! I'm home.

GEPPETTO (*To audience*): Pinocchio is *all boy*! (*To* PINOCCHIO) Hello, Pinocchio. How was school today?

PINOCCHIO: Terrible! They wanted me to add two numbers together, underline pronouns, and print the state capitals on a U.S. map ... and that's hard!

GEPPETTO: I guess school is just not the place for wooden heads.

PINOCCHIO: Oh, I don't know. The teacher said a lot of the boys have wooden heads.

GEPPETTO: Tell me, isn't there anything you like about school?

PINOCCHIO: Sure! Stick ball! (SHIRLEY *enters.*)

SHIRLEY (*Sweet and sugary*): Hello, everybody. I'm home! Just relax while I run back to the kitchen and cook supper. Then you two can play a game of checkers while I wash the dishes. O.K.?

GEPPETTO: That's fine, but why don't you let us help you? Haven't you been working hard at school all day?

SHIRLEY: Oh, no! School is fun! We learn to iron sleeves, sew zippers, wash out grease spots and bake bread!

PINOCCHIO: See! What they have girls do is easy!

SHIRLEY: Then after school I took my violin lesson, attended a Shakespeare reading, tried out for the cheerleading team, joined the Needlepoint Club, and picked up six orders for dolls out here in front of the workshop. If business gets any better, you'll have to hire extra help!

PINOCCHIO: After school I played in the mud! (MOD-MOTHER *enters.*)

MODMOTHER: Hey, shazam, flimflam, and alakazam! It's me again, your very own personal, genuine, one and only Fairy Modmother!

GEPPETTO: Oh no! Time to decide!

MODMOTHER: Right on! Which will it be: The bright, sweet, considerate, helpful Shirley? Or (*Points to* PINOCCHIO *who is still slouched in chair*) ... him?

GEPPETTO: But I like them both!

MODMOTHER: Do you mean that the girl can be equal?

GEPPETTO: Equal is not the way they do things — but the way I *feel* about them is equal.

MODMOTHER: Far out and heavy thinking, wise one. For that, you get not one, but two — count 'em, two real, live persons. (*Points wand at* PINOCCHIO *and bell sounds*)

PINOCCHIO: That's funny! Now that I'm a real, live boy I feel different. (*Puts finger to temple*) The square root of 729 is 27. In Spanish "to eat" would be *como, comes, come, comemos, comeis, y comen;* and if you —

GEPPETTO: Wonderful, wonderful! And now his sister!

MODMOTHER (*Pointing wand at* SHIRLEY, *as bell sounds*): Ah-h-h-h, the sweet sound of liberation!

GEPPETTO: At last you're a real girl. Now I'll always have someone to clean, cook and make beds.

SHIRLEY: No way! You and Pinocchio had better learn to clean, cook and make those beds yourselves. I've decided to accept an offer to become Editor of *Junior Ms.:* "The Mag That's Your Bag." (*Rolls down jeans, which have been concealed under dress, pulls off ruffled skirt and blouse which has sweater under it, and puts on hat*) I'll be back at six. Have supper ready — we'll talk about what's happening in the publishing business. (*Exits*)

GEPPETTO: My, that's some change!

MODMOTHER: That's the way things are now in today's real world.

PINOCCHIO: Don't worry, Papa. I'll always stay with you. (*Turns away and quickly puts on long nose, then turns to face* GEPPETTO, *displaying nose*) I'll never, never leave home!

GEPPETTO: Look! His nose — it's growing!

MODMOTHER: So? (*Shrugs; to audience*) Today things change so fast that even I can make a mistake! (*Curtain*)

THE END

Good as Goldilocks

Say the secret word ...

Characters

Goldilocks
Papa Bear
Uncle Groucho Bear
Mama Bear
Baby Bear
Narrator

Setting: *Kitchen in home of Three Bears.*
At Rise: *Stage is empty.*

Narrator (*Entering*): The story you are about to see is true — every bit of it. That is, it's true that every bit of it is a story. It's about a family called the Three Bears and a sweet young thing called Goldilocks, and how she came looking for porridge that was *just right.* As the story opens, the Bears are about to come downstairs to eat. (*Exits*)

Mama (*Entering*): Oh, my goodness, I should have the

porridge served by now. Papa Bear will be down soon, and if it's not ready, he will be like a bear all day. (*She takes three bowls — small, medium, large — off mantel and sets three places. She then gets large cooking kettle from fireplace and stands ready to dish out porridge with large wooden spoon. Calling*) Soup's on! Come and get it! (BABY BEAR *enters swiftly and heads straight for table.*)

BABY BEAR: O-boy, o-boy, o-boy, o-boy, o-boy . . . (*He repeats this until he is sitting in small chair at table with napkin tucked under chin, holding silverware upright in both hands.*)

PAPA BEAR (*Sauntering in casually*): Soup's on, eh? Big deal. Odds are it'll be *too hot.*

BABY BEAR: I'll bet it will be *just right.* (PAPA *scowls at* BABY's *enthusiasm as he takes his place by large bowl and reaches for large serving kettle which* MAMA *is holding. She raps his hand with spoon.*)

MAMA: You know we never start until everyone is seated.

PAPA (*Rubbing hand and blowing on knuckles*): How could I forget! (MAMA *slowly walks to opposite end of table and carefully places large kettle in center.*)

MAMA: There.

PAPA (*Sarcastically*): On second thought, it won't be *too hot.* By the time we eat, it will have ice on it!

MAMA (*Sitting*): Now (PAPA *again reaches for kettle*) — before we begin (PAPA *stops and sits frozen in reaching position until she finishes.*) — I want to tell you some good news!

PAPA (*Turning head to look at audience*): We're not finally going to eat, are we?

MAMA: No, we're going to have a visitor today.

PAPA (*Sitting back in chair*): Not Goldilocks again?

BABY: Uh-oh! There goes my chair!

MAMA: No, not Goldilocks — Uncle Groucho Bear is coming to spend some time with us.

BABY (*Happily*): Uncle Groucho! Yippee!

PAPA: Uh-oh! There go my cigars!

MAMA: Now, that's no way to talk about Uncle Groucho! After all, he's the most photographed bear in all of Yellowrock National Park.

PAPA: He's just a big ham.

BABY: I like him!

MAMA: Why, he even made the cover of *American Wildlife.*

Papa: Only because it showed Smokey the Bear stamping out Uncle Groucho's cigar.

BABY: I think he's *just right.*

MAMA: Think of all the children who imitate his every move — his every word.

PAPA: When our son imitated his words, you washed his mouth out with soap.

MAMA: Please keep in mind that he is my mother's only brother.

PAPA: But does he have to visit us again?

MAMA: Keep in mind that he is also very *rich.*

PAPA: Oh yes, rich! (*Smiles at audience*) Come to think of it, he's really not so bad, after all.

BABY: Remember last time he was here and he pulled your tie?

PAPA: I remember.

BABY: Then he said it was too long?

PAPA (*With disgust*): I remember!

BABY: Then he got the scissors and cut it off? (*Laughs*)

PAPA: I remember! I remember! (*More disgusted*) I was wrong. He really *is* that bad! (*To* MAMA) When is he coming?

MAMA: I'm not sure.

PAPA: You mean there's a chance that he's *not* coming?

MAMA: No, it's just that his telegram said "Arriving tomorrow," and I'm not sure when he sent it.

PAPA: Telegram! I'm surprised he would spend the money for a telegram — even to let us know he was coming to sponge off us for two or three weeks!

MAMA: Well . . . he sent the telegram collect. . . .

PAPA: It figures.

MAMA: And he also said he could stay until Christmas.

PAPA: Why didn't I believe my horoscope when it said to stay in bed?

BABY: I like Uncle Groucho. I think he's *just right*. (PAPA *looks at* BABY *with disgust, then at audience, then drops his head against table and raps it several times against top.*)

PAPA: Why me? Why me?

MAMA: Now we've talked so long that the porridge is cold. (*Picks up kettle and stands*) Come on, I'll put this back on the fire while we go for a nice walk in the woods. (*Places kettle on fireplace*)

BABY: Oh, boy, a walk in the woods. That sounds *just right*! (*Stands and moves toward exit with* MAMA)

PAPA (*Standing*): Who knows? Maybe I'll be hit by a

falling tree and will have to go to the hospital —
until Christmas. (*Exits, followed by* BABY *and*
MAMA. *After a moment, knocking is heard from
offstage.*)

GOLDILOCKS (*Calling, from offstage*): Hello! Is anybody home? Yoo-hoo! (GOLDILOCKS *enters.*) Mama
Bear! Papa Bear! Baby Bear! (*Walks to table*) This
must be the place — a big bowl for Papa Bear, a
middle-sized bowl for Mama Bear, and a little teensy
bowl for Baby Bear. Let's see now, I'm supposed to
taste from the little bowl, then the big bowl, then —
no — it's the other way around. I should start with
the big bowl. (*Sits at* PAPA'*s place, takes spoon*)
What's this? The bowl is empty! (*Looks into other
bowls*) They're all empty! How can I do this right if
all the bowls are empty? (UNCLE GROUCHO BEAR
*enters, walking in bent-over, striding fashion, imi-
tating Groucho Marx. He clasps "cigar" behind
back.*)

GROUCHO: You want something? Just try me. (*Wiggles
oversized eyebrows at audience*)

GOLDILOCKS (*Amazed; staring*): What?

GROUCHO (*Pacing about*): Say the secret word and
collect fifty bucks.

GOLDILOCKS: Secret word? All I want to do is taste the
porridge, and —

GROUCHO: That's the secret word. Pay the winner fifty
bucks (*Wiggles eyebrows at audience*) — and throw
in fifty squaws, too, if it suits your papoose.

GOLDILOCKS (*Shaking head*): I'm confused. Who are
you?

GROUCHO: Well, Confused, I'm Groucho Bear, and believe me, I'd be confused, too, with a name like yours.

GOLDILOCKS: Oh, no! I don't mean my name is confused. My name is Goldilocks.

GROUCHO: Well, I should hope so, for your sake. I once knew a bright young girl named Informed. They called her Miss Informed — and, come to think of it, she was confused, too.

GOLDILOCKS (*Standing*): Oh, now I don't know what to do. According to the story, you're not supposed to be here!

GROUCHO: Well, don't tell me, tell my mother, or better yet, tell my boss.

GOLDILOCKS: All I know is that I'm supposed to come into the Three Bears' house (*Crossing to door and back*), taste the porridge from the big bowl and say, "This porridge is too hot," then taste from the middle-sized bowl and say, "This porridge is too cold," then taste from the little bowl and say, "This porridge is just right."

GROUCHO (*Wiggling eyebrows*): Say the secret word and everything will be *just right.*

GOLDILOCKS: But the bowls are empty! Now what do I do?

GROUCHO: If you knew that, you wouldn't be here. (*Indicates audience*) But neither would they. Small loss either way.

GOLDILOCKS: Now I remember what to do. (*Moves* PAPA's *chair from table to center stage*) Chairs! I'm supposed to say (*Sitting in chair*), "This chair is much too big!" (*Gets* MAMA's *chair and puts it beside* PAPA's) And then, "This chair is still too big." (*Gets* BABY's *chair*) "And this chair is *just right.*" (*Jumps up and down in chair*) Then it's supposed to break. (*Stops, exasperated*) Nothing is working right today. (*To* GROUCHO) Will you help me?

GROUCHO: Well, now, never let it be said I didn't help a lady. (*Pushes* PAPA's *chair to table and fills bowl from kettle*) Not that I will help . . . I just don't want it to be *said* that I didn't. (PAPA, MAMA *and* BABY *re-enter.*)

BABY: Hey, look! Uncle Groucho is here!

GROUCHO: You're right! Now, say the secret word and collect fifty bucks — but, tell everyone to bring his own doe.

BABY (*Laughing*): Uncle Groucho, you're funny!

GROUCHO: And you're Baby Bear, but who's this with you? (*Looks closely at* PAPA)

BABY: That's my dad — Papa Bear! Don't you remember?

GROUCHO: I never forget a face — but in his case I could make an exception.

MAMA: Well, look who else is here — Goldilocks! (GOLDILOCKS, *frightened, jumps up from chair and runs to far corner.*) I'll get some more bowls, and we can all have a picnic. (*To* GOLDILOCKS) Can you stay and eat with us? (*Begins setting more places*)

GOLDILOCKS (*Timidly coming forward*): What are we . . . eating?

MAMA: Why, porridge, of course.

GROUCHO: Good idea! Say, did I ever sing, "But, Oh,

How That Woman Could Cook"?

PAPA (*With disgust*): Repeatedly!

GROUCHO: Good, then you already know just how sickening it is. Come to think of it, her cooking wasn't much better. She was probably confused. Or maybe she was Miss Informed . . . but that's another story.

GOLDILOCKS: Somehow this just doesn't seem to be the way it happens in the story.

MAMA: Soup's on! Come and get it!

BABY: O-boy, o-boy! (*Grabs his chair, takes it to table, sits, tucks napkins in neck and holds silverware up.*)

GROUCHO (*Mimicking* BABY): O-boy, o-boy! (*Goes to table in same manner as* BABY *and sits at* MAMA's *place*)

PAPA (*Moving to table and taking his place*): The way my luck is running, it will be my chair that breaks — with me in it!

GOLDILOCKS: Maybe next time I should try out for Little Bo Peep. Surely a story about lost lambs couldn't be so mixed up.

GROUCHO: Let's try it. I'd like to be a sheep and pull wool over your eyes.

MAMA (*Starting to dish porridge from kettle*): Oh, no! It's been on the fire too long. Now it's too hot!

BABY: Why don't we go for another walk in the woods? When we come back it will be *just right.*

PAPA: Not again! (*Lets head drop to table as before.*)

MAMA: Yes, a walk in the woods will work up our appetites.

GROUCHO: Work up an appetite? Now that's the most

ridiculous thing I ever heard.

GOLDILOCKS (*Moving toward fireplace*): Oh, well, this looks like a good chance to earn a cooking badge. (*To* BEARS) Why don't you all just sit down and let me fix something to eat? I got a blue ribbon for my honey cakes at the County Fair.

ALL BEARS (*In unison*): Now that sounds *just right*. (*Curtain*)

THE END

Let's Hear It for the Pied Piper!

An old-time treat to a modern beat . . .

Characters

LORD MAYOR, *who wants to rid Hamelin of rats*
FIRST COUNCILOR, *who wants to become Lord Mayor*
SECOND COUNCILOR, *who always speaks with a question*
THIRD COUNCILOR, *who always carries oversized book and quill pen*
CHRISTINA, *the Lord Mayor's daughter*
PIED PIPER, *a cool, kazoo-carrying free spirit*

SETTING: *Council Room in Town Hall of Hamelin. Exit is at one side. A large open window above courtyard is in wall opposite. There is a long table in center. Crests, other ornaments are on walls. There is a large, black safe in one corner.*

AT RISE: COUNCILORS *stand to one side in conversation.*

LORD MAYOR (*Entering*): Gentlemen, we must do

something about the rats! The people of Hamelin are gathered in the square! They are up in arms!

1ST COUNCILOR: Tax collecting, road supervision, and ceremonial functions — these are the duties of the Councilors.

2ND COUNCILOR: Did you select us — the Honorable Councilors — to be rat exterminators?

3RD COUNCILOR (*Checking pages of large book and speaking pompously*): Section One, Paragraph Seven of the township ordinance defines the duties of the —

LORD MAYOR: But everywhere I go there are rats! And everywhere I go the townspeople are complaining! If we do not do something about the rats very soon, I will not be re-elected, and I will not be able to appoint *you* three as councilors.

1ST COUNCILOR (*Changing tone from haughty to pleasant*): You are quite right about the rats. You may rest assured that we have been concerned — most concerned. (*Other* COUNCILORS *nod heads in approval.*) So let me take this opportunity to tell you that we have extended our duties and formulated a plan to rid the town of rats.

2ND COUNCILOR: Did you think we would not find a solution?

3RD COUNCILOR: It is already in the book. (*Pats book lovingly*)

1ST COUNCILOR: Now, please step outside and make a public announcement. Tell the townspeople that the plan will be put into effect very soon.

LORD MAYOR: I knew you three would not fail me in this time of crisis. These are not the times for a sunshine soldier or a summer patriot; these are the times that try men's souls. I know not what —

1ST COUNCILOR: Yes, very nice. Just make the announcement outside to the townspeople.

LORD MAYOR: Yes, yes! Of course! (*Exits*)

2ND COUNCILOR: Plan? Did you say we had a plan?

3RD COUNCILOR (*Leafing through book*): I didn't record any plan.

1ST COUNCILOR: That's because there is no plan.

2ND COUNCILOR: No plan? Didn't you just say —?

1ST COUNCILOR: I know what I said! Somebody had to say something! You heard the Lord Mayor. The townspeople are "up in arms"!

2ND COUNCILOR: Do you mean we are going to practice a little deception?

3RD COUNCILOR (*As though quoting book*): Deception: the act of deceiving; to cheat; a fraud.

1ST COUNCILOR: Yes, the Lord Mayor is just now announcing that he has a plan to rid Hamelin of the rats. If we come up with an idea and it does get rid of the rats, then *we* will claim the credit and I'll be elected next Lord Mayor.

2ND COUNCILOR: Was it not written by our famous founding father, Franklin Benjamin, that, "Deception is the best policy"?

1ST COUNCILOR: Now, on the other hand, if we cannot get rid of the rats, we can blame it on the Lord Mayor's plan, and then I'll be elected next Lord Mayor.

2ND COUNCILOR: Doesn't that sound like "Heads you win, tails you win"?

3RD COUNCILOR (*Patting book*): You can make book on it.

LORD MAYOR (*Entering*): Now, what is this plan? The townspeople have accepted my word that we could—

CHRISTINA (*Enters running*): Daddy, Daddy! I just heard about the plan. How wonderful! When will it be put into effect? When will we be rid of the rats?

LORD MAYOR: Later, Christina. We are still working on it.

CHRISTINA: Yes, but I can hardly wait! Give me a hint, will you? Just one small hint? Please?

LORD MAYOR (*Impatiently*): These things take time! Now run along so we can get to work on it.

CHRISTINA: All I want to know is when we'll be rid of the rats, and how we'll be rid of the rats, and who will —

LORD MAYOR: *RATS!* That's all I hear! I'd give a thousand guilders to rid Hamelin of rats!

PIED PIPER (*Entering; speaking in "cool" manner*): Oooooooooeeeee! Like, man, I hear you calling!

LORD MAYOR (*To* COUNCILORS): Who . . . is that?

PIPER: I am the Pied Piper, Head Dude, and where I lay the beat, the vibes will freak your mind.

LORD MAYOR: What is he saying?

1ST COUNCILOR: He said he was beat.

2ND COUNCILOR: Didn't he say he was a freak?

3RD COUNCILOR: Let me check the book! (*Leafs through pages*)

PIPER: Ooooohhhhh-oh! (*To* CHRISTINA) Do these cats always hang square ears on you?

CHRISTINA: I'm afraid so, but they mean well. You

see, we're having a terrible time with rats.

PIPER: Like I know — I know! That's why I made the scene. Lay a thousand guilders on me and I will take up this gig and *ZAPPO!* — the rats will *mi-grate, dis-si-pate,* and *eeeeeee-vac-u-ate!*

1ST COUNCILOR: Sir, if you have a complaint, please secure the proper forms for obtaining an appointment during office hours.

2ND COUNCILOR: Do you think the Lord Mayor can take time to talk with just anyone who drops in?

3RD COUNCILOR: Section Four, Paragraph Six of the Procedures Section —

CHRISTINA: But, he's saying he can get rid of the rats!

1ST COUNCILOR (*To other* COUNCILORS): I thought he said he could make scenes.

2ND COUNCILOR: Didn't he say he could lay on a thousand guilders?

3RD COUNCILOR: I can't find any of that in the book! (*Turning pages frantically*)

PIPER (*To* CHRISTINA): Man, like I'm picking up no vibes at all from them. To rap with this group is to *ir-ri-tate, ag-gra-vate,* and *suuuuuuf-fo-cate!*

CHRISTINA: Wait, I know! He's your plan, isn't he, Daddy — the plan to rid Hamelin of rats! Oh, Daddy, you're a genius!

1ST COUNCILOR (*Exchanging knowing glances with other* COUNCILORS): Genius is right! Here we were working on a much less effective idea and our great Lord Mayor already had his own brilliant plan.

2ND COUNCILOR: Is he not truly a genius?

3RD COUNCILOR: I shall put it in the book. (*Writes with pen*)

LORD MAYOR: No! He's not ... I mean (*Pauses and smiles*) — genius? Well, yes — *YES!* He is the plan! (*To* PIPER) See here, young man, if we should decide to offer you the job, how soon could your services be implemented?

PIPER: You mean when? Man, like now! I will *pen-e-trate, cul-ti-vate,* and *exxxxxxx-tri-cate!*

1ST COUNCILOR (*To other* COUNCILORS): That's strange — penetrate.

2ND COUNCILOR: Cultivate?

3RD COUNCILOR: I'm looking, I'm looking! (*Leafs through book again*)

PIPER: Just lay out the bread, man, 'cause I will be right back.

LORD MAYOR (*To* CHRISTINA): He wants bread?

CHRISTINA: No, he wants you to get the money ready — the thousand guilders.

LORD MAYOR: Oh yes, of course, my good man. You shall have it upon completion of the task.

CHRISTINA: Well, Mr. Piper, the job is yours. How are you going to do it?

PIPER: The only way to do any gig, little lady, is with the rock vibes of music. (*Puts kazoo to mouth, plays any popular melody, prances around stage, and exits.*)

CHRISTINA (*Watching* PIPER *as he exits*): Look, Daddy, the rats *are* following him! They really are!

LORD MAYOR (*Looking*): So they are. They're coming out from everywhere!

1ST COUNCILOR: Look! He's leading the rats right out of the city!

2ND COUNCILOR: Does that tell us something about his music?

3RD COUNCILOR: This is one for the book! (*Begins writing*)

CHRISTINA: I've got to see where he's taking them. Do you want to come along?

LORD MAYOR: Yes. (*To audience*) Many voters will be watching. (*To* COUNCILORS) Get the money ready so we can pay him immediately upon his return. (*Exits in a rush behind* CHRISTINA. 2ND *and* 3RD COUNCILORS *bow low.*)

1ST COUNCILOR (*Walking up center and stroking chin reflectively while* 2ND *and* 3RD COUNCILORS *are still bowing*): A thousand guilders . . .

2ND COUNCILOR (*Straightens up, as does* 3RD COUNCILOR): It was a thousand guilders, wasn't it?

3RD COUNCILOR (*Checking book*): It is so written.

1ST COUNCILOR (*Continuing as though thinking out loud*): One thousand guilders . . . to rid our town of rats.

2ND COUNCILOR: Is something wrong?

3RD COUNCILOR: Not with my books!

1ST COUNCILOR (*Still facing audience, but now expression becomes obviously devious*): A thousand guilders to rid our town of rats? Look around you, gentlemen. (*They do so, slowly.*) Do you see any rats?

2ND COUNCILOR: Do you mean do *I* see any rats? (*Continues looking*)

3RD COUNCILOR (*Recites from book*): Rats, gnawing animals, usually gray, black, or brown with small beady eyes and long hairless tails. (*Looks up from book and around stage as though seeking rats*)

1ST COUNCILOR: No! They are all gone! You do not see a single rat! So . . . I submit, gentlemen, why should we pay a piper one thousand guilders to rid our town of a nuisance that no longer exists?

2ND COUNCILOR: Do you mean we shouldn't pay the Piper at all?

3RD COUNCILOR: But I wrote it in the book!

1ST COUNCILOR: Oh? You wrote it in the book? Let me see. (*Looks at book*) Now you see it (*Rips out page*) . . . and now you don't. (*Smiles at audience as he crumples page and tosses it over shoulder*) Remember, to be a politician, you have to practice a little deception.

PIPER (*Entering in swinging manner*): Ooooooooeeeee! Like *con-grat-u-late, em-u-late,* and *cel-l-l-l-e-brate!* The rats are busted and it's heavy-heavy time!

CHRISTINA (*Entering behind* PIPER): Oh, Councilors, it's wonderful! The Pied Piper has taken away all the rats. Now our city will be beautiful again!

1ST COUNCILOR (*To other* COUNCILORS): The Lord Mayor's daughter says it is a Pied Piper.

2ND COUNCILOR: Oh? And what does he want?

3RD COUNCILOR (*Checking book*): Audiences are granted on —

CHRISTINA: He wants his money — the thousand guilders — for taking away the rats!

1ST COUNCILOR: Oh, the rats. First we must meditate.

2ND COUNCILOR: Innovate?

3RD COUNCILOR (*Writing*): And calculate.

PIPER: Oh-oh. That's the lead to a jive cop-out if ever my ears were tuned.

1ST COUNCILOR: I do not intend to lead a "jive."

2ND COUNCILOR: Did he say "get a cop out"?

3RD COUNCILOR (*Looking in book*): Police are listed under Section Five, Paragraph —

CHRISTINA: He said you were not going to pay. (*To* PIPER) Oh, no, Mr. Piper, you're mistaken. They're going to pay. You took away the rats just as you said you would.

1ST COUNCILOR (*To* PIPER): Am I to understand you want money?

PIPER: You've got it, Clyde.

2ND COUNCILOR: How much was this sum to be?

CHRISTINA: You *know* it was a thousand guilders!

3RD COUNCILOR: I see nothing in the book — nothing!

CHRISTINA: I was here! I heard you agree to pay him one thousand guilders.

1ST COUNCILOR (*Moving to* PIPER, *putting hand on his shoulder, affecting great concern, and leading him toward exit*): I'll tell you what: We are honorable men. Bring your contract to the next council meeting and we will, in good faith, pay whatever amount it states.

CHRISTINA: Contract! But he didn't get a contract!

1ST COUNCILOR: No contract? (*Smiles at other* COUNCILORS) Did you say "No contract"?

PIPER: Hey, man, like, I feel a rip-off coming!

CHRISTINA (*To* COUNCILORS): Surely you must be joking! It was just a short time ago. We all stood right here in this very spot and you agreed to pay one thousand guilders to Mr. Piper to rid our town of rats!

PIPER: Cool it, little lady. They have plans to *hes-i-tate, vi-o-late,* and *in-n-n-n-val-i-date!*

CHRISTINA: But, Mr. Piper, they promised! A promise is a promise! (*To* COUNCILORS) Just wait until my father hears about this!

PIPER: Let's bug off. There are other ways. (*Takes out kazoo and smiles while holding it ready to play*) There are *other* ways. (*Exits with* CHRISTINA)

1ST COUNCILOR: Gentlemen, you were perfect! You have this day saved Hamelin one thousand guilders!

2ND COUNCILOR: Should not our prudence be rewarded?

3RD COUNCILOR: Section Eight, Paragraph Three of the Gratuities Code states that, "Rewards should be bestowed upon those good citizens who render service to their city."

1ST COUNCILOR: A very good code, yes. I think we deserve ... ah, say, a thousand guilders!

2ND COUNCILOR (*Smiling*): Apiece?

3RD COUNCILOR (*Smiling broadly*): I'll write it in the book. (*He writes. All watch. Then* 1ST COUNCILOR *crosses to safe, opens it, and begins to count out money.*)

LORD MAYOR (*Entering*): Ah-h-h-h-h! The rats are gone, the townspeople are happy, and we can, at last, get down to business as usual. First item (*Sitting at table*), did you take care of the Piper?

1ST COUNCILOR (*Pocketing the money so* LORD MAYOR *will not see*): Your Lordship (*Smiling at other* COUNCILORS), I would say we took care of the Piper quite nicely.

2ND COUNCILOR (*Smiling smugly*): Is not a promise a promise? (*All three are giggling at their own cleverness.*)

3RD COUNCILOR: I have it listed under "*R*" for rewards.

LORD MAYOR (*Standing and slamming fist on table in rage*): Then why is the Piper standing outside right now with my daughter, who says you *refused* to pay him?

CHRISTINA (*Entering with* PIPER): That's right, Daddy. They said he didn't have a contract.

LORD MAYOR: That's because it was a gentleman's contract. Something they wouldn't know anything about. (*To* COUNCILORS) Councilors, it's time we paid the Piper. (*Holds out hand for money, which* COUNCILORS *take from pockets and hand to him*) But, Mr. Piper, didn't our contract call for you to rid Hamelin of *all* the rats? (*Looks at* COUNCILORS)

PIPER: Right on, Head Dude, I see three I missed. (*Takes kazoo and plays as he cavorts and dances around stage.*)

1ST COUNCILOR (*Following* PIPER): Help, my feet won't stop!

2ND COUNCILOR (*Also following in awkward skip dance*): Can't we talk this over?

3RD COUNCILOR (*Dancing in similar fashion*): I can't even write in the book! (*All move toward exit.*)

LORD MAYOR: Wait, Piper. Your thousand guilders (*Looks at money*) — plus a well-deserved bonus. (PIPER *exits with* COUNCILORS *dancing behind.*)

CHRISTINA: I'll take it to him, Daddy. After all, the next tune he plays will be the Wedding March. (*Curtain.*)

THE END

Sleeping Beauty Wakes Up

Tall tale about a short king . . .

Characters

KING
MERLIN THE MAGICIAN
SIR ELROY
SLEEPING BEAUTY
REBEL
TWO GUARDS

TIME: *Long, long ago.*

SETTING: *Throne room of King. There is a throne center, with a tasseled cord hanging on wall nearby. There is an arched window in wall, with a coat of arms beside it.*

AT RISE: SIR ELROY *is leaning on throne, napping.* REBEL *enters, crawling stealthily, concealing large cardboard sign behind back. Sign reads,* THE KING IS A SHORTY. *He tiptoes to throne and places sign on throne. He steps back to admire it, then starts to exit right.* KING *enters right, coming face to face with* REBEL, *who does an about-face and hurries left.*

KING: Halt! (REBEL *turns, frightened, his knees knocking, and kneels before* KING. ELROY *wakes with a start.*)

REBEL: Your Majesty!

KING: Quiet, you! (*Calls*) Guards! (TWO GUARDS *march in and salute with arm across chest.*)

GUARDS (*Together*): Yes, sire?

KING: As your King, I command you to return that rebel to the dungeon and add five years to his sentence! (TWO GUARDS *march to* REBEL. *Each takes one of his arms. They drag him toward exit.*)

REBEL (*Incredulously*): Life ... *plus five years?* (*They exit.*)

KING (*Moving to throne, tearing up sign, and throwing it away*): The King is a shorty, eh? (*To* ELROY, *who is still half asleep*) And just where were you when that man escaped from my dungeon and boldly entered my throne room?

ELROY: I was ... well, you see, I just —

KING: You were asleep, that's what you were! (*Sits on throne*) The King is a shorty! So that's what they all say behind my back. (*Looks over shoulder*) So what? History is full of great men who were short. Isn't that true, Sir Elroy?

ELROY (*Coming to attention awkwardly*): Oh, yes, sire. There was ... ah ... Let's see ... well, how about ... ah ...

KING: I'm waiting!

ELROY: Hm-m-m ... Maybe you're the only one, sire.

KING: I'm tired of being the only one who is short. I'll summon Merlin the Magician (*Pulls cord near throne*) and demand that he make me tall! (*There is a puff of smoke from offstage and* MERLIN *enters in a flurry. A smoke pot may be used.*)

MERLIN: Shazam! I, Merlin the Magician, appear in a flash through magic.

KING (*Standing*): Good wizard, I have a job for you.

MERLIN: Wizard? Sire, please, I'm a magician, not a wizard.

ELROY: Just what is the difference, anyway?

KING (*Sarcastically*): A magician uses two more rabbits per performance.

MERLIN: Sire! A wizard uses tricks; a magician uses magic.

KING: O.K., so use some of this magic and make me tall.

MERLIN: Come again?

KING: Tall — I want you to make me tall!

MERLIN: Gadzooks! You don't want magic, you want a miracle!

KING (*Angrily*): Come again?

MERLIN: I said, miracle. (*Thinking fast*) It's a miracle. Only last night I had a dream ... ah ... in which all your subjects looked up to you.

KING: Really? All my subjects ... looked *up* to me? (*Throws shoulders back and stands straight*)

MERLIN (*Stalling*): Yes, sire ... You see, in this dream — this vision — you went upon a great quest and found a queen!

KING: A queen! (*Sits*) I don't like it already.

MERLIN: Hear me out, sire. Not just any queen, but

one whose beauty is known throughout the land. All the world will look up to the king who makes Sleeping Beauty his queen.

KING: Who?

MERLIN: Sleeping Beauty, sire. Hast thou not heard of Sleeping Beauty?

KING: Not since I was five years old.

ELROY: I heard about her only yesterday!

KING: It figures.

MERLIN: But, sire, she exists! Take my word as a magician. Singing swords, frogs into princes — that's my stock-in-trade.

KING: Hm-m-m. (*Walks downstage away from throne as he speaks*) Find Sleeping Beauty and make her my queen so my subjects will look up to me ... I don't know. It doesn't sound too promising. (REBEL *enters stealthily, unnoticed. He carries a sign reading,* THE KING IS A SHRIMP. *As he starts to put it on throne,* KING *turns and sees him.*) Halt!

REBEL (*Miming frustration at being caught, then turning, dropping to knees and pleading*): Sire, I —

KING: Guards! (TWO GUARDS *march in and salute.*) Return that man to the dungeon and add five years to his sentence!

GUARDS (*Together*): Yes, sire! (*They drag* REBEL *toward exit as before.*)

REBEL: Life ... plus five years ... *plus five more years?* Couldn't you just send me to bed without my supper? (*Exits with* GUARDS)

KING (*Tearing up sign*): That does it! Sir Elroy, I am

going on a quest with the Magician to find Sleeping
Beauty. I want you to come along to protect us from
the hazards of uncharted lands.

ELROY: Hazards?

KING: The perils of a foreign terrain.

ELROY (*Backing away one step*): Perils?

KING: The dangers of fierce wild animals.

ELROY (*Taking another step back*): Dangers? Sire, I
can't go. I just remembered that my new suit of
armor has a defect in it.

KING: So, just keep the visor down and nobody will
notice. Now go, both of you, and prepare! We leave
at sunrise! (*Curtain*)

*   *   *   *   *

SCENE 2

TIME: *The next day.*

BEFORE RISE: REBEL *peeks out from under curtain,
smiles at audience, then crawls cautiously out from
under curtain, glancing left and right. He brushes
dirt from clothing. He holds up sign reading* THE
KING IS A RUNT *and prepares to attach it to curtain.
Suddenly curtain opens.*

SETTING: *A forest, with cardboard bushes and trees.
Entrance to cave is at left, and a sign at entrance
reads* QUIET ZONE. SLEEPING BEAUTY AT REST. DO
YE NOT DISTURB.

AT RISE: REBEL *is about to attach sign to curtain as
curtains open. He stands there frightened as* KING,

SIR ELROY *and* MERLIN, *at center, glare at him.* MERLIN *is carrying a large cauldron.* ELROY *wears armor.*

KING: Guards! (TWO GUARDS *march in and salute.* REBEL *turns to audience with anguished look on his face, tears up the sign, and pretends to eat it.*) Return that man to the dungeon and add five years to his sentence. (GUARDS *take* REBEL*'s arms and drag him toward exit.*)

REBEL: Life ... plus five years .. plus five years ... *plus five years?* The turnkey will put in for overtime! (*Exits with* GUARDS.)

KING: Well, now, Magician, where is this Sleeping Beauty?

MERLIN (*Setting cauldron down*): Sir Elroy, read the directions I worked out with the magic incantation. (ELROY *fumbles through pockets and finally comes up with a piece of paper.*)

ELROY (*Reading*):
> My lance is broken.
> My sword is bent.
> My horse is lame.
> My quest is spent.
> I'm a lonesome knight tonight.

(*He looks puzzled.*)

MERLIN (*Grabbing paper away*): You read the wrong side, imbecile! Those are the lyrics to my new country-and-western song.

KING: Cut the commercials and just tell us where Sleeping Beauty is!

ELROY: Look, a cave! (*Points to cave entrance, left*)

MERLIN (*Crossing to cave*): Yes, this is it. Here at the entrance is a sign. (*Reading*) "Quiet Zone. Sleeping Beauty at Rest. Do Ye Not Disturb." (*Looks at others and shrugs*) And down at the bottom it says, in fine print (*Reading*), "In case of awaking Sleeping Beauty, directions for putting her back to sleep are as follows: "Recite incantation 47, chant 3, while intoning 'Sleep, sleep.'" Hm-m-m. That's funny. (*To* KING) Why would they give instructions for putting her back to sleep?

ELROY (*Crossing to sign*): What's that in small print?

MERLIN: Way down here? (*All gather around sign.* REBEL *enters unnoticed, right. He carries a sign reading,* THE KING IS A MIDGET.) I can't make it out. It looks like "Beware . . ."

REBEL (*Looking alarmed, then hiding behind "bush" so that he is concealed from* KING, MERLIN *and* ELROY *but not from audience; in loud, commanding voice, through sign rolled into megaphone*): Beware! Beware! All who trespass here become the victims of the curse of the colossus. (*Laughs to himself*)

KING (*Facing direction of voice*): An attack! Quick, Sir Elroy, prepare for countermaneuvers! (ELROY *drops to knees, lowers head, and extends sword above head with both hands.*) Sir Elroy! What countermaneuver is that?

ELROY: Surrender, sire!

REBEL (*So amused he can barely compose himself*): Get up, you miserable mite! I want you, that stunted magician, and especially that squirt of a king to be standing tall — at least as tall as possible — when I step on you! (*He laughs to himself.* KING *at first cringes in fear, then puts hands on hips angrily and approaches bush concealing* REBEL.) If there's one thing I can't stand, it's a puny, undersized, microscopic monarch! (KING *pushes bush aside.* REBEL *is mugging so enthusiastically to audience that he does not realize he has been discovered.*) Ready or not, here I — (*He sees* KING.) Uh-oh! (*He starts to crawl away.*)

KING: Halt! Guards! (GUARDS *march in and salute.*) Return that man to the dungeon and add three years to his sentence.

REBEL (*As* GUARDS *drag him toward exit as before*): Three years! Only three years! At this rate I could be out by 1776! (*Exits with* GUARDS)

MERLIN: Now, sire, let us get on with our quest for Sleeping Beauty.

KING: I can hardly wait.

MERLIN: Sir Elroy, let us venture forth into the cave and get our new queen.

ELROY (*Peering in*): But it's dark in there.

KING: So, why do you think I brought a knight? Go!

ELROY: Yes, sire. (*Exits into cave.* MERLIN *starts to follow, then steps aside just at the opening and remains onstage. From offstage*) I can't see a thing. Oops!

SLEEPING BEAUTY (*From offstage, speaking loudly and precisely without pausing*): Well, at last a prince has come. It's about time! What kept you? Step back. I can get up by myself. Look at you! Your armor is a mess — rusty, squeaky.

ELROY (*Offstage*): But —

SLEEPING BEAUTY (*Offstage*): Don't "but" me. You should know better than to come spell-breaking in an outfit like that. (MERLIN *and* KING *cast furtive glances at each other and slowly back away from cave.*)

ELROY (*Offstage*): But —

SLEEPING BEAUTY (*Offstage*): And stand up straight! Are you supposed to be a tall, handsome prince or just a paltry peasant?

ELROY (*Offstage*): But I'm not a prince, I'm —

SLEEPING BEAUTY (*Offstage*): Not a prince, eh? (*She enters, wearing cone hat and scarf and long gown slit to reveal boots and shorts. She walks directly to* MERLIN.) I should have known that in this so-called man's world a prince would send someone else to do his work for him. (*To* MERLIN) Look at your hair! (*Walks around him*) It's a mess! And that ridiculous hat has got to go. (ELROY *re-enters and stands upstage.*)

MERLIN: But —

SLEEPING BEAUTY: Don't interrupt! Just listen. Pray tell, just what kind of prince would wear moons on his nightgown?

MERLIN: But, I'm not a prince! There *is* no prince! But, there is ... a king! (*Points to* KING)

SLEEPING BEAUTY (*Looking in direction of* KING, *but over his head.* NOTE: KING *should be standing close to her*): Where?

KING (*Disgusted*): Here!

SLEEPING BEAUTY: Oh, down there.

KING (*To* MERLIN): This is *not* what I had in mind!

SLEEPING BEAUTY: Oh, it isn't, is it? I suppose you thought it would be all that fairy-tale and romance stuff — sweep me off my feet and live happily ever after. Just like a male chauvinist! No, sirree! We will be an equal-opportunity family. None of that lying around, thinking I'm going to feed you grapes. Let me tell you, I'm a liberated woman! Whatever you can do, I can do (*Looks down at him with contempt*) ... probably better!

MERLIN (*Moving toward cave to look at sign; to himself*): What was it that put her back to sleep? Oh, yes, incantation 47, chant 3! (*Holds up hands in mystical fashion*) Sleep, sleep!

SLEEPING BEAUTY: Hey, none of that! I — (*She drops her head, makes snoring sounds, and exits into cave, her arms extended trance-like in front of her.*)

KING: Well, Merlin, any more bright ideas?

ELROY: My father always said one should learn from one's mistakes.

KING: Yes, I see his point. You're an only child, aren't you?

MERLIN (*Pondering*): I've got it, sire — the perfect solution! (*Gestures mystically toward cauldron.*) Hocus, pocus. Alakazam! (*Reaches in, pulls out tall crown, removes* KING's *crown and places tall one on* KING's *head*) Well, sire, how do you like that? (*REBEL enters and runs quickly across stage, handing* KING *a sign that says,* THE NEW KING IS A BEANPOLE. *He exits before anyone onstage can react.*)

ELROY (*After all have read sign*): Beanpole! Sire, this is an outrage. I'll have the rebel's head for that!

KING (*Smiling at sign*): His head? ... No, he shows signs of promise. We'll knight this man and appoint him my Royal Press Secretary! (*Curtain*)

THE END

Hansel, Gretel & Co., Inc.

A "crumby" tale

Characters

NARRATOR
HANSEL
GRETEL
MAMA
PAPA
FAIRY GODMOTHER
WITCH

SCENE 1

BEFORE RISE: NARRATOR *enters in front of curtain.*

NARRATOR: This is the story of Hansel and Gretel. Now, if you recall, Hansel and Gretel are two delinquents who run away from home, stay out after curfew, vandalize an old lady's home, and, when they are caught, throw her into the oven. *"Horrible!"* you say, and we agree. However, with the current crackdown on media violence, the story today would be more like this. (*Exits as curtain opens*)

SETTING: *Kitchen of Hansel and Gretel's cottage. Wooden table and chairs are at center, with a fireplace and cupboard at back. Many old-fashioned brooms are scattered around the room. Door is at left.*

AT RISE: HANSEL *and* GRETEL *are seated at table, making brooms.*

HANSEL: I'm hungry.

GRETEL: You're always hungry.

HANSEL: But, Gretel, it's almost four o'clock and we haven't eaten since lunch.

GRETEL: So, who cares? I'm on a diet, anyway. Girls have to be selective about what they eat.

HANSEL: Yeah, but I'm a boy, and I'm hungry.

GRETEL: Oh, Hansel, can't you think of anything else but food?

MAMA (*Entering with a sack*): Hello, children. I'm home. (*Sets down sack and takes off scarf*)

HANSEL (*Rummaging in sack*): Did you bring something to eat? I'm hungry!

MAMA: You're always hungry.

HANSEL (*To audience*): What is this, an echo chamber?

GRETEL: Did you have a good day at the market, Mama?

MAMA: Heavens, no! The prices are outrageous! Eggs, seven cents a dozen; milk, three cents a quart; and a sack of flour was a dime! However, I did find a good buy on napkins. (*Takes napkins from* HANSEL, *who has just taken them from sack*) See — they match our wallpaper!

HANSEL: Napkins? I'm starving, and she worries about kitchen decor!

GRETEL: Oh, Hansel, be patient. Papa will be home soon, and if he sold any brooms we'll have plenty to eat. (HANSEL *sits and slumps in seat.*)

MAMA: Tell me, Hansel, were you a good boy today, and did you make your daily quota of brooms?

HANSEL: I made seventy-five brooms. Yesterday I made seventy-five brooms. The day before I made seventy-five brooms. The barn is full of brooms, the smokehouse is full of brooms, the cellar is full of brooms. It would take a countrywide cleaners' convention to unload all those brooms!

MAMA: Just keep making them, Hansel. You know what your papa says — "Someday brooms will sweep the country."

GRETEL: Let's go down by the well and wait for Papa to come.

HANSEL: I have a better idea! Let's go into the forest and pick strawberries — nice, big, juicy, red strawberries! Mm-m-m-m! (*Rubs stomach and smacks lips*)

GRETEL: Oh, no! We can't do that!

MAMA: Hansel, you know the forest is bewitched and that anyone who goes in *never* comes out again.

HANSEL: Maybe they decide to stay and eat strawberries rather than sit at home and starve.

GRETEL: No, they say an old witch lives in the forest!

HANSEL: Whoever lives there, I'll bet they eat more than we do. I'm hungry.

MAMA *and* GRETEL (*Together*): You're always hungry!

HANSEL: There you go again! Can't you ever say anything else?

GRETEL: Can't you ever be anything else but hungry?

PAPA (*Entering*): Hello. I'm home, and guess what? I sold two brooms today!

HANSEL: Big deal. At that rate, by the end of the year we'll have only 26,270 brooms — plus the brooms in the barn, the smokehouse and the cellar. (*Takes sack held by* PAPA) What did you bring to eat?

PAPA: Nothing. You should see those prices! They wanted six cents for a pound of butter and three cents for a dozen apples! So, I bought some more string to make brooms.

HANSEL (*Holding up string, then dropping it back into sack*): So I noticed. I'm going into the forest and pick some strawberries before I faint and waste away from starvation. (*Exits*)

GRETEL: Wait! (*Moves toward door*)

MAMA: No, Hansel! (*Takes loaf of bread from cupboard*) Quick, Gretel, go after him. Break up this bread and leave a trail of crumbs to follow home. (GRETEL *takes bread and exits.*)

PAPA: Strawberries? Sounds good! Maybe I should have bought some cream. (*Curtain*)

*　　*　　*　　*　　*

SCENE 2

BEFORE RISE: NARRATOR *enters in front of the curtain.*

NARRATOR: In Scene 1 Hansel ran off into the forest

and Gretel went to find him. What will happen? Will they both get lost? Will the witch get them? Will they ever get home again? Will their father get some strawberries? Mm-m-m-m. Strawberries! That does sound good! On with the show. (*Exits as curtains open.*)

SETTING: *A forest.*

AT RISE: *Stage is empty, then* HANSEL *trudges in slowly.*

HANSEL: Whew! Walking in the forest is hard work. I'm tired. (*Wipes perspiration from forehead*) And I'm hungry!

GRETEL (*Offstage*): You're always hungry.

HANSEL (*Startled*): Who said that? (GRETEL *enters.*)

GRETEL: I did, silly. I've been trying to catch up with you ever since you left home.

HANSEL: But why? I thought you were afraid of the big, bad witch.

GRETEL: Well, I am, but Mama sent me after you with some bread to see that you get home all right.

HANSEL: Bread? Bread! Hey, I didn't know we had any bread! Give it to me. I'm hungry. (*Reaches out*)

GRETEL: The bread is all gone.

HANSEL: Gone! Do you mean you ate it?

GRETEL: Heavens, no. I can't eat bread on my diet. Too many calories. I broke it up and left a trail of crumbs for us to follow home. See! (*Points offstage*) Right along there where the birds are.

HANSEL: You nincompoop! You can't leave a trail of bread crumbs. The birds are eating them!

GRETEL: Oh, no! Now we *are* lost! We'll never find our way home.

HANSEL: Home! Who wants to go home? I'm still looking for strawberries. I'm hungry!

GRETEL: You're always hungry.

FAIRY GODMOTHER (*Offstage*): Presto-chango, alaka-zam! I'm here in a flash to help you.

HANSEL (*To* GRETEL): Did you hear something?

GRETEL (*Frightened*): Yes, but where did it come from?

GODMOTHER (*Offstage*): Right over here.

HANSEL: Right over where? I don't see anybody!

GODMOTHER (*Offstage*): Over here by the ... the ... Oh, dear, I forgot to make myself visible. (*Steps on-stage*)

HANSEL: Visible? (*They see her.*)

GRETEL: Oh, no! It's the witch! (*They cower together.*)

GODMOTHER: Witch? Did someone say witch? Where? (*Cowers with* HANSEL *and* GRETEL)

GRETEL: Aren't you the witch?

GODMOTHER: Me? A witch? Don't be ridiculous! I'm a fairy godmother. See, I have a wand. (*Searches for wand, which she cannot find. Audience can see it tucked under arm.*) Now where did I put that thing?

GRETEL: A fairy godmother?

GODMOTHER: Yes! I'm a fairy godmother. And you must be Cinderella all ready to go to the ball and meet the Prince — but, wait! Who is he? (*Points at* HANSEL)

HANSEL: I'm Hansel.

GODMOTHER: Hansel? You don't belong here. Shoo!

Go away. What would the Prince say if he knew Cinderella was here with you?

GRETEL: But I'm not Cinderella. I'm Gretel, and Hansel is my brother.

GODMOTHER: Hansel and Gretel! But I'm supposed to meet Cinderella. Do you know where she lives?

HANSEL: There's no Cinderella in our neighborhood. She must live on the other side of the forest.

GODMOTHER: Good, then that's where I'll go. I'll just wave my wand and ... (*Continues search*)

GRETEL: Here (*Indicates under arm*), is this it?

GODMOTHER: Yes! Now, abracadabra-Kalamazoo, hocus ... hocus ... Oh, dear, how does that go?

HANSEL: I don't know. Now, what about us?

GRETEL: We want to go home!

GODMOTHER: Home? I don't know anything about home. How about a nice magic mirror? Or frogs! I'm very good at changing frogs to princes ... or is it pumpkins? But not now. I've got to find ... ah ... what's-her-name? (*Sticks wand in hair behind ear*)

GRETEL: Cinderella.

GODMOTHER: Yes, Cinderella, and help her get ready for the whatcha-ma-call-it.

GRETEL: Grand ball.

GODMOTHER: Whatever. But if there is anything I can do for you, just let me know, and I'll take my wand and ... Now where is that wand? (*Searches her own pockets, etc.*)

GRETEL: Here! (*Shows her*)

GODMOTHER: I'll take my wand, and presto! It's yours.

HANSEL: In that case, how about strawberries?

GODMOTHER: Right now I have to find (*Exits right; from offstage*) what's-her-name —

GRETEL (*Calling*): Cinderella.

GODMOTHER (*Offstage*): Yes, Cinderella. Cinderella. I've just got to remember that name. Cinderella, Cinderella (*Fading*), Cinderella, Cinderella...
(WITCH *enters left, unobserved. She carries a small strawberry plant.* HANSEL *and* GRETEL *are looking right, after* GODMOTHER.)

WITCH: The boy wants strawberries, he'll get strawberries! Heh, heh, heh! (*Puts plant down*) Won't he be a tasty morsel! (HANSEL *and* GRETEL *turn.*) Whoops! Time for a hasty exit! (*Exits*)

GRETEL: Do you think the Fairy Godmother will find poor Cinderella in time?

HANSEL: Poor Cinderella! What about us? I'm — (*Sees strawberries*) I'm looking at strawberries! Fresh, ripe, juicy, red strawberries! I didn't see these before. Come on, let's eat! (*Begins eating*) Mm-m-m!

GRETEL: Wait, Hansel! This might be some kind of trick the witch is using.

HANSEL (*Still eating*): Best-tasting trick I ever ate. Try some.

GRETEL: But I'm on a diet. Oh, well (*Begins picking berries*), the best thing about a diet is that you can always start tomorrow. (*Eats*)

HANSEL: Wow! Those were good! Let's just lie back now and rest. I'm ... (*Lies down*) I'm sleepy ... (*Sleeps*)

GRETEL (*Yawning*): That's funny, I thought you were always hungry ... (*Also sleeps. Curtain*)

*   *   *   *   *

SCENE 3

BEFORE RISE: NARRATOR *enters in front of curtain.*

NARRATOR: Scene 3 takes place in the forest, which is the same place as the last place they shouldn't have been in the first place. Now if you remember, Hansel and Gretel have fallen asleep. Will they become slaves to the Wicked Witch? Or will they be saved by the . . . the . . .

GRETEL (*From offstage*): Fairy Godmother!

NARRATOR: Yes, Fairy Godmother, who will wave her . . . her . . .

GRETEL (*From offstage*): Wand!

NARRATOR: Wand. Let us surmise no longer. Scene 3 begins. (*Exits as curtains open.*)

SETTING: *The same as Scene 2. Candy house is now up right.*

AT RISE: HANSEL *and* GRETEL *are sleeping.*

GRETEL (*Stretching and yawning*): What a dream I had! (*Sits up*) All about being lost in the forest and . . . (*Looks around*) Oh, no! We *are* lost in the forest and (*Sees candy house*) something is different! Hansel! (*Shakes* HANSEL, *who does not move.*)

HANSEL: I'm asleep.

GRETEL: Hansel, wake up! We're lost in the forest!

HANSEL (*Still not moving*): Leave me alone.

GRETEL: Hansel, we're lost, and a suspicious-looking house has appeared overnight!

HANSEL: Tell it to come back later.

GRETEL (*Looking frightened*): Oh, Hansel, wake up

... (*To audience*) I know what will get him up. (*To* HANSEL) Hansel, are you hungry?

HANSEL (*Sitting up immediately*): Yeah, how did you know?

GRETEL: Because you're always — never mind. Look! (*Points at house*)

HANSEL: Hey, yeah! Peppermint windows! (*Stands*)

GRETEL: Where did it come from? (*Stands*)

HANSEL (*Starting toward it*): Gingerbread shingles!

GRETEL: How did it get here?

HANSEL: Chocolate doors!

GRETEL: Hansel, don't touch it. (HANSEL *eats a piece of the house.*) I just know it can't be good.

HANSEL: Good? Not good? (*Eating*) You're right, it's not good. (*Takes more*) It's delicious. Have some.

GRETEL: Oh, why not? Didn't I say I would start on my diet tomorrow? (*Also eats*)

WITCH (*Entering left, opposite house*): Nibble, nibble, nibble ...

HANSEL: Did you say something? (*Continues to eat*)

GRETEL: I said my diet could start tomorrow.

HANSEL: No, I mean something that sounded like —

WITCH (*Moving closer*): Nibble, nibble.

GRETEL: No, I didn't say — (*Sees* WITCH; *screams*) The witch!

WITCH: No, not the witch. I'm the wicked, evil, terrible, vile, diabolical witch!

HANSEL (*Still eating*): Boy, this is a great place you've got here.

WITCH: You like it? Good! Heh, heh, heh. Keep right on eating and get round, and plump, and tasty.

GRETEL: Hansel, stop! She's going to fatten us up and

eat us. Let's get out of here. (HANSEL *does not move except to eat.*) Help! Help!

WITCH: Yell all you like, you silly girl. There is no one around to hear you.

GRETEL: Help! Mama! Papa! Fairy Godmother! Anybody!

GODMOTHER (*Entering*): Presto-chango, alakazam! I'm here in a flash to help you.

GRETEL: Thank heavens! Save us from this wicked, evil, terrible, vile witch!

WITCH: You forgot diabolical.

GRETEL: This wicked, evil, terrible, vile, diabolical witch, who wants to fatten us up and eat us, and all we want to do is pick strawberries and go home. Please!

GODMOTHER: Strawberries? Go home? Witch? (*Looks at* WITCH) Agnes? Is that you? What are you doing to these children?

WITCH: Oh, nothing, really. I just wanted to give them a little scare before sending them home. One has to practice now and then to keep up the image. If you don't keep at it, you start slipping, you know.

GODMOTHER: Goodness, do I know!

WITCH: I've been wanting to zip off to the Senior Witches' Retirement Home, but I broke my broom and I can't go anywhere.

HANSEL: Broom? You want a broom? We have hundreds of brooms.

WITCH: Where?

HANSEL: At our cottage, near the entrance to the forest.

WITCH: Wow! How about a trade? I'll trade you the

whole forest for all your brooms.

HANSEL: It's a deal!

WITCH: Good. (*Hands "deed" to* GRETEL) Here's the deed. (*To audience*) Now I won't have to bother with children at all except maybe on, heh, heh, heh, Halloween. (*Exits; from offstage*) Heh, heh, heh . . .

MAMA (*Entering with* PAPA): Look, Papa, it's Hansel and Gretel! We've found them!

PAPA: Do they have the strawberries?

GRETEL: Mama! Papa! (*Rushes to meet them*) Look! We just traded the witch all our brooms for the whole forest. (*Shows deed*)

HANSEL: Including this candy house. (*Begins eating*)

PAPA: I always knew that boy would eat us out of house and home.

MAMA: No, I'd say he ate us *into* house and home this time! (*Curtain*)

THE END

Snow White and Friends

A fairy tale spoof

Characters

Narrator
Queen
Snow White
Mirror
Woodsman
Doc
Dopey

Scene 1

Setting: *The Queen's throne room.*

At Rise: Mirror *is placed near throne. The* Narrator *enters and addresses the audience.*

Narrator: The story you are about to see is about a little girl who, just overnight, grew up and became beautiful. Her name is Snow White, which gives you a clue to the time and setting. As the scene opens, we see the wicked Queen. (Queen *enters, yawns, wanders to throne, and sits.*) She has just banished three knights, dispossessed four rich merchants, beheaded two commoners, and now she is looking for more fun things to do. Having found no one around, she turns to her faithful Magic Mirror. (QUEEN *goes to* MIRROR.) And with that, dear audience, I take my leave. (NARRATOR *exits.*)

QUEEN: Tell me, Mirror, am I not still the most lovely and desirable creature that ever lived?

MIRROR:
>   To hear the things I have to say,
>   You must ask the proper way.

QUEEN: Oh, good heavens! You and your ridiculous rhymes! When are you going to give up the idea that you're some kind of Edgar Allan Poe and just be a plain old looking glass?

MIRROR:
>   A looking glass is all I can be,
>   When you forget to question me.

QUEEN: Oh, all right! All right!
>   Mirror, mirror on the wall,
>   Who's the fairest of them all?

MIRROR:
>   Raven hair as soft as silk,
>   Eyes so bright and blue,
>   Blushing sunshine in her cheeks,
>   A heart so kind and true;
>   The radiance of her tender smile,
>   The countenance of a saint;
>   All these things of loveliness —
>   Too bad — *you* it ain't!

QUEEN: Your jokes are even worse than your grammar.

MIRROR:

> There are some things, O my Queen,
> Of which I joke a lot,
> But where your beauty is concerned,
> You *know* I kid you not!

QUEEN: What? For someone to be lovelier than I is out of the question. It's treason! It's even very bad manners! Tell me who it is!

MIRROR:

> A lovely sight —
> Young Snow White.

QUEEN: Snow White? You're putting me on. She's just a little girl, an adolescent, a mere child!

MIRROR:

> Once a child was our Snow White.
> But she grew up — just overnight.

QUEEN: I can't have this. She must be eliminated. I'll hail the knights! I'll summon the guard!

MIRROR:

> No, no! My dear Queen,
> You don't want attention.
> This foul deed must come to pass
> Without your slightest mention.
> Call in some obscure person,
> From a far-off, wooded plain.
> Have him rid you of this girl,
> Then send him back again.

QUEEN: Very good! Sometimes you're worth every penny I spend on polish. (*Calling offstage*) Summon the Woodsman from his far-off, wooded plain.

WOODSMAN (*Entering immediately*): You summoned?

QUEEN: Yes. What kept you? I have a little chore for you.

WOODSMAN: Chopping down trees?

QUEEN: Well, it's a kind of chopping.

WOODSMAN: Name it, O Queen. It shall be done.

QUEEN: You see, there's this girl who thinks she's more beautiful than I. She's not, of course, but if she keeps saying she is, someone will think my subjects do not always deal in the truth, as does their Sovereign Queen.

WOODSMAN: Perish the thought.

QUEEN: No, not the thought — it's Snow White who must perish.

WOODSMAN: Snow White? Little Snow White? But she's just a child . . . a little girl!

QUEEN: That was yesterday. She grew up — just overnight.

WOODSMAN: You realize that disposing of girls is not really my line of work.

QUEEN: Silence! You have a choice between two heads.

WOODSMAN: Two? One was plenty!

QUEEN: A choice between two, Woodsman. Yours or the girl's. Well?

WOODSMAN: When you put it that way, it narrows down the selection.

QUEEN: Quit stalling and get out there and do your job.

WOODSMAN: Very well, my Queen. (*Bows and leaves*)

QUEEN: Heh, heh, heh! (*To* MIRROR) How about that, Mirror-Mirror-on-the-wall? (*Curtain*)

*   *   *   *   *

Scene 2

Setting: *The forest. A stump is down center.*
At Rise: Narrator *enters and sits on stump.*

Narrator: As we say in the theatre, the plot thickens. What will happen to young Snow White, who grew up overnight and became beautiful? Can the wicked Queen make it hot enough to melt the snowy beauty of Snow White? We'll find out in the second scene. Here are the Woodsman and Snow White in the forest. (Woodsman *and* Snow White *enter.*) Snow White is unaware of the Queen's evil intentions. She thinks that the Woodsman has brought her into the forest to broaden her knowledge of conservation and to show her the natural resources of their fair country. (Narrator *exits and* Woodsman *and* Snow White *come down center as the* Woodsman *points out trees to her.*)

Woodsman: And this, Snow White, is a fir tree of the genus *Abies.* It is a coniferous pine that yields lumber and resins.

Snow White: Oh! How very interesting.

Woodsman: And now, if you will bend over this stump, you can see what's over here.

Snow White (*Bending over stump and looking off*): Way over here?

Woodsman: Yes. (*Prepares ax*) That's it. Now hold it. (*He hesitates, then drops ax.*) I can't do it! I just can't do it!

Snow White: Can't do what, Mr. Woodsman?

Woodsman: The Queen's dirty work. She sent me out

here to get rid of you because you are more beautiful than she is.

SNOW WHITE: Me? Beautiful? Why, only yesterday they were calling me the Ugly Duckling.

WOODSMAN (*Gloomily*): That was yesterday. (*Brightening*) Look, I'll tell you what. You stay here in the woods and I'll go back and tell the Queen you're dead.

SNOW WHITE: Will that be safe for you, Mr. Woodsman?

WOODSMAN: I'll be all right. The Queen's getting old. It won't be too long before many girls will be more beautiful than she is, and you'll be able to come back.

SNOW WHITE: Whatever you say, Mr. Woodsman.

WOODSMAN: Don't call me "Mr. Woodsman." My name is Boswell Smith.

SNOW WHITE: Whatever you say, Mr. Boswell Smith.

WOODSMAN: No! Not "Mr." — just Boswell — Boswell!

SNOW WHITE: Whatever you say, Boswell-Boswell.

WOODSMAN (*Shrugging*): Whatever *you* say, Snow White. Now I must go. Be careful in the woods. (*Exits*)

SNOW WHITE (*Waving*): Thank you and goodbye. Now, which way shall I go? (*Looking off right*) That sign over there says, "To Grandma's House." That's the wrong story. If I remember correctly, I'm supposed to find some dwarfs who'll take care of me.

DOC *and* DOPEY (*Chanting off left*): Hi-ho, hi-ho. (*They enter.*)

DOC: Man, it's like off to work we go.

SNOW WHITE: Oh! Who are you?

DOC (*To* DOPEY *as he sees* SNOW WHITE): Cease and desist, we've found the skin man.

DOPEY: Groovy. (*They go up to* SNOW WHITE *and look at her closely.*)

DOC: Say, Dopey, dig that crazy costume he's wearing.

SNOW WHITE (*Looking around*): He?

DOPEY: Like yeah, man.

DOC: Hey, Dad, where are your sticks?

SNOW WHITE: Sticks?

DOC: Skin-tappers, pace-setters, the 2-4's. How can you make your skins cry without your beaters?

DOPEY: Like, yeah, man.

SNOW WHITE: Beaters? Skins? I don't know what you're talking about!

DOC: You know, Dopey, like I have a feeling this cat's not our man.

DOPEY: I don't even think it is a man, Doc.

DOC: Yeah? (*Walks around* SNOW WHITE) Yeah! It's all that long hair. I thought it was a boy.

SNOW WHITE: I'm Snow White. I'm looking for some dwarfs.

DOC: Dwarfs! That's us! You must be that skin man!

SNOW WHITE: What's a skin man?

DOC: That's a drummer. (*To* DOPEY) We're not only playing in different keys, but one of us is like playing the wrong tune. Communicate, Dopey.

DOPEY: O.K., Doc. (*To* SNOW WHITE) You are Snow White — we are the Dwarfs.

SNOW WHITE: You don't look like dwarfs to me. Aren't

dwarfs supposed to be little men?

Doc: We grew up. Even Peter Pan must be an old man by now.

Snow White: All I know is that I'm supposed to meet the Seven Dwarfs and they will take me home and help me.

Dopey: That's our *name:* "The Seven Dwarfs — Littlest Band with the Biggest Beat." He's Doc, and I'm Dopey.

Doc: So, like, who put you on to us?

Snow White: Nobody. It's just the way the story goes: The Wicked Queen wants me eliminated because she thinks I am more beautiful than she is.

Doc: The Queen! Now, why didn't you say so? Anyone on the Queen's list can't be that square. Are you sure you can't play drums?

Snow White: I'm sure. (*Crying*) Oh-h-h, why does the Queen hate me so?

Dopey: Cool it, kid. The Queen doesn't like us either.

Doc: The Dwarfs had three discs on the top ten and were slated for TV and personal appearances all over the kingdom. But the Queen fixed that.

Dopey: We were getting to be more popular than the Queen.

Snow White: Did she try to kill you?

Doc: No. She like sentenced us to a new kind of "wild" life. (*Indicates surroundings*) Now we blast for the creatures of the forest ... the sparrows and the blue jays.

Dopey: The Queen said our playing was for the birds.

Doc: Are you *sure* you're not a drummer?

SNOW WHITE: I'm really quite certain. Now, can't we go? It's getting dark.

DOC: Say, maybe the little lady's a go-go dancer.

SNOW WHITE: Absolutely not! However, I did sing in the church choir.

DOC: Man, that's it! A singer! Now, that could give our sound some real class. (*They start to exit together*) Let's hear you try a few bars of "I Dream of Queenie with the Light Brown Throne." Start at the beginning and give it all you've got. (*They exit as curtains close.*)

* * * * *

SCENE 3

SETTING: *The Queen's throne room.*

AT RISE: MIRROR *is beside throne.* NARRATOR *enters.*

NARRATOR: For the next scene we go back to visit the Queen and her magic mirror. If you recall, it was the mirror that started this whole mess in the first place, by telling the Queen that Snow White had grown up overnight, and had become more beautiful than she. Now you *know* that a mirror with a mouth like that is going to snitch on the Woodsman. What will happen? Will Snow White remain in the forest and sing lead for the Dwarf Combo? Will the woodchopping Woodsman be caught and given a taste of his own chopping? Or, will he escape to the woods and become the new drummer for the Seven Dwarfs, Littlest Band with the Biggest Beat? Anticipate no longer. (*He indicates* QUEEN, *who has just entered, then exits.*)

QUEEN: Ho-hum, another day, another ten thousand dollars. I wonder who that brilliant monarch was who discovered taxes. It certainly makes being a queen tolerable. (*Looks in* MIRROR) What is this? A wrinkle? Oh, no! I'm getting old! It's all this worrying I've been doing about Snow White. I wonder if I could tax people for giving me wrinkles? Oh, wait! It's only a hair brushed across my cheek. What a relief! (*Pauses to admire herself*) What a doll I am. There can never be anyone to equal my great beauty. Isn't that right, Mirror?

MIRROR:

To hear the things I have to say,
You must ask the proper way.

QUEEN: Oh, brother! One of these days, one of these days — *pow!*

MIRROR:

Just remember if you do,
It's seven years' bad luck for you.

QUEEN: Don't push me! Sometimes I think it would be worth it.

MIRROR:

Let's hear your question one more time,
And, if you please, recite in rhyme.

QUEEN: All right, all right. (*Hastily*) Mirror-mirror-on-the-wall-who's-the-fairest-of-them-all?   Now, hurry up and tell me.

MIRROR:

    Sometimes you go too far, my Queen.

    My patience can be spent.

    You can always be replaced by

    An elected president.

QUEEN: Quit stalling. Now, get on with it!

MIRROR:

    I'll get on with it, my dear,

    But you won't like what you will hear.

QUEEN: Just stick with facts, and never mind the opinions.

MIRROR:

    Raven hair as soft as silk,

    Eyes so bright and blue,

    Blushing sunshine in her cheeks,

    A heart so kind and true;

    The radiance of her tender smile —

QUEEN (*Interrupting*): Wait a dog-bone minute! You're not going to give me that Snow White routine again, are you? Get with it. Remember? The Woodsman? (*Chops imaginary ax*)

MIRROR:

    Snow White is very much alive,

    Our lovely heroine.

    The tenderhearted Woodsman was

    Too kind to do her in.

    She's taken refuge with some dwarfs,

    Who helped her in her plight.

    Now she's singing groovy tunes

    With the disco band each night.

QUEEN: Snow White is still alive! That chicken-hearted Woodsman! Those crazy dwarfs. I'm their Queen! Where's all the respect for Her Royal Majesty? The dignity of the Traditional Monarchy? What's a queen to do when her subjects don't obey her?

MIRROR:
> Beauty is not meant to be
> One's only goal in life.
> It's courage, faith, and goodness
> That can take life's toil and strife.
> These things will stay right with you,
> They can't be bought or sold.
> Beauty withers with the years,
> And, face it, Queen — you're old.

QUEEN: You stupid old mirror! You just say that because you're not as pretty as I am.

MIRROR:
> I just reflect what faces me;
> I think Snow White should be left free.

QUEEN: Do your reflecting somewhere else. I must do some thinking. Let's see now. I must get rid of Snow White myself. Certainly can't trust men to do anything! (*Strolls back and forth*) I know! I'll poison her. I'll take this nice, big, red, juicy (*Pulls banana from pocket*) — banana? Oh, well, one thing will work as well as another. Heh, heh, heh! An apple a day keeps the doctor away — a banana brings the undertaker. Ha! Ha! Ha! (*To* MIRROR) How about that, Mirror-Mirror-on-the-wall? (*Curtain*)

*   *   *   *   *

SCENE 4

SETTING: *The forest.*
AT RISE: NARRATOR *enters.*

NARRATOR: Well, there you have it — everything but the finale. As this scene opens, the Queen has disguised herself as an ugly, old woman. (QUEEN *enters*) And now . . . (*Sees* QUEEN) Say, I thought you were supposed to be an ugly old woman.

QUEEN: Heaven knows I tried, but it's very hard to disguise this great beauty of mine.

NARRATOR (*Shrugging*): Whatever you say, Queen. The Queen has disguised herself as a *beautiful* old woman and has brought the poisoned banana to give to Snow White, hoping she will eat it and drop dead. (*He exits.*)

QUEEN: Oh, Snow White — where are you? Yoo-hoo! Come out, come out, wherever you are! (SNOW WHITE *enters.*)

SNOW WHITE: Were you calling me?

QUEEN: Yes. You're such a cute little thing and do such a marvelous job singing with the band, I want you to have this banana. (*Offers it to her*)

SNOW WHITE: No, thank you. You've been to the club to hear me?

QUEEN: Yes, I've been to the club. I used to do some singing myself. Here, have a banana.

SNOW WHITE (*Taking banana*): You're a little old to be a go-go girl, aren't you?

QUEEN: It was back in the Golden Era of Big Bands. We used to jitterbug to the boogie-woogie.

SNOW WHITE: Jitterbug? Boogie-woogie? My, you don't look *that* old! (*Hands back banana*) I really don't care for this banana.

QUEEN: But it's such a beauty and I *do* want you to have it. (*Gives banana back to her*)

SNOW WHITE: Well, all right. But I still don't like bananas.

QUEEN (*Smiling*): This one is ... different. (SNOW WHITE *peels it and takes bite, then she drops to floor.*) Heh, heh, heh! Let's see you sing now! Ha, ha, ha!

DOC (*Entering with* DOPEY): Hey, Granny-o, what's all the giggling about?

QUEEN: Well, hello! Who are you?

DOC: Doc Dwarf, leader of the coolest sound this side of the Ming Dynasty.

QUEEN: Cool sound? You sell noisy refrigerators?

DOC: No, Ancient Square One. The Seven Dwarfs, Swinging-est Disco Sound in the Kingdom.

QUEEN: The Dwarfs!

DOPEY: You know our music?

QUEEN: I've heard it (*To* DOC), but I sure didn't know it was led by such a handsome, mature gentleman.

DOC: You're kind of cute yourself. What say we split this scene and get acquainted? (*Takes apple from pocket*) Would you care for this juicy, red fruit?

QUEEN: A pleasure, Mr. Dwarf. (*Accepts apple, starts to eat. They exit.*)

DOPEY: Hey, like what about me? (*Shrugs, turns and sees* SNOW WHITE *still on floor*) Holy Hullabaloo! What's wrong with Snow White?

WOODSMAN (*Entering*): She is waiting for me!

DOPEY: Like that?

WOODSMAN: Sure, it's an old story. The Queen just gave her a poisoned banana and I'm the Prince with the remedy that will get her back on her feet in no time. Let's see — (*Searches pockets, finds bottle*) Toad Turner. No, that's not it. (*Takes out another bottle*) Here it is! Anti-Banana. (*Passes bottle under* SNOW WHITE*'s nose*)

SNOW WHITE (*Sitting up abruptly*): Wheeew! What's that smell? It must be my Prince. (*Rubs eyes*) Wait, you're not the Prince — you're the Woodsman.

WOODSMAN: Wrong! I am the Prince disguised as a Woodsman to escape from the Queen. But that's all ended now.

SNOW WHITE: Is she dead?

WOODSMAN: No, better than that. Doc just gave her a Boy Scout Apple.

SNOW WHITE: What's a Boy Scout Apple?

WOODSMAN: One bite and it will make her trustworthy, loyal, helpful, cheerful, thrifty, brave, clean, reverent. Also, she will feel like doing a good deed every day! (*Curtain*)

THE END

Aladdin Strikes It Rich

When wishes come true . . .

Characters

ALADDIN
ALADDIN'S MOTHER
HASSAN
MAGIC LAMP
JEANIE
NARRATOR

SCENE 1

BEFORE RISE: NARRATOR *enters in front of curtain.*

NARRATOR: This story takes place during the time of the Arabian Nights. That was many, many years ago, way back before television. In fact, it was so long ago, it was even before radio. Just ask your parents or teachers how long ago *that* was! It is about Aladdin and the Magic Lamp. As our story opens, we see young Aladdin and his mother sharing the good times of hard times. (NARRATOR *exits as curtain opens.*)

SETTING: *Aladdin's house, with stone walls, window, cupboard, crude tables and chairs, fireplace with kettle.*

AT RISE: ALADDIN'S MOTHER *is pacing in front of fireplace.* ALADDIN *is seated at table.*

ALADDIN'S MOTHER: Aladdin, you are a lazy, lazy boy! If you don't get a job soon, we're going to starve.

ALADDIN (*Protesting*): Ah-h-h-h, Mom!

MOTHER: You think I'm kidding? Look at the cupboard! There's not even a bone for the dog!

ALADDIN: Come on, this isn't Mother Hubbard we're doing. It's Aladdin. Remember? Any time now a stranger will come and take me to get the Magic Lamp. . . . Then we'll have three wishes and live happily ever after.

MOTHER: Ha! Three wishes! What I think about are the *three jobs* you were offered this past week. And you didn't take any of them.

ALADDIN: That's because none of them suited my work potential, my monetary expectations, or my predicted future advancement.

MOTHER: What you mean is that they all called for WORK!

ALADDIN: Ah-h-h-h, Mom!

MOTHER: Stop that "ah-h-h-h, Mom" stuff. Tomorrow morning I want you up and out of here at the crack of dawn to check on the job offer with that nice Ali Baba. With forty positions open, you have a good chance.

ALADDIN: Ah-h-h-h, Mom!

HASSAN (*Entering quickly, speaking in overdramatic manner of politician*): Here I am, Hassan the Great, Predictor of the Future!

MOTHER: Now wait a minute, whatever-your-name-is! What makes you think you can burst in here without knocking?

HASSAN: Knocking? (*Turns and knocks with much animation*) There, you want knocking, you get knocking.

ALADDIN: He's right, Mom. That's knocking!

MOTHER: But we didn't hear it until he was already inside, you brainless blockhead.

ALADDIN: Ah-h-h-h, Mom!

HASSAN: Your mother is absolutely right. I entered before I knocked because I, Hassan the Great, can predict the future. I see all, hear all, know all!

ALADDIN: Wow! Hear that, Mom? The future! That means he's going to take me to get the Magic Lamp!

MOTHER: Humph! He sounds like a used-carpet salesman to me.

HASSAN (*Ignoring comment and continuing, covering eyes in mystic way*): I knew that in this house lives a small boy with (*Peeks through hand*) brown hair. And he lives with his (*Peeks again*) mother.

ALADDIN: That's right! That's us! We've lived here for a long time! You really can predict! I can hardly wait to get my hands on that Magic Lamp!

MOTHER: I still say he's selling carpets.

HASSAN (*Continuing with flourish*): I also knew that if I presented myself at your front door, you would bid me, "Come in."

ALADDIN: That's right again! That's what we say! Let's go get that Magic Lamp!

MOTHER: First he'll show us his carpet samples.

HASSAN: After you bid me, "Come in," I would enter and stand much as I am standing now. Then, I would call straight to you, my lad. I would call, "Ahmed ... Ahmed." I would say, "I am here to —"

ALADDIN: Ahmed? My name is Aladdin! Aladdin! Surely you know that. Remember? Aladdin and the Magic Lamp?

MOTHER: Some predictor of the future he is. He doesn't even know your name. Even a carpet salesman would get that right. Out! (*Starts to push* HASSAN *toward exit.*) Out!

HASSAN: Wait. (*Turns back to* ALADDIN) Do you really think I don't know your name? I laugh. Ha, ha! (*With theatrics*) Of course I, Hassan the Great — the Predictor, who sees all, hears all, knows all — certainly I know your name. It is Aladdin. I spoke it in the tongue of the Ancient Seers in which Aladdin translates into Ahmed, and means ... ah ... "One of Great Wit."

MOTHER: Well, I'd say the Ancients were about half right.

ALADDIN: We're wasting time! When are we going to go get the Magic Lamp?

HASSAN: Now you should know I am here to — (*Changing tone from dramatic and mystic to curious*) Lamp? Did you say *Magic* Lamp?

ALADDIN: Sure, you know, the Magic Lamp that you

came here to take me to find, and when we get it, it will give us three wishes and we'll become rich and happy? Remember, you have to use me because I'm small enough to wriggle into the cave. Come on! We're still wasting time!

HASSAN: But, I came here to sell you ... (*With sudden interest*) "Magic Lamp," you say? Three wishes? Come, my boy, haste is always an essential ingredient of any quest. We must be off. (*Exits with* ALADDIN)

MOTHER: That's a new way to get rid of a carpet sales-man. But, we must give him credit. He was right about one thing ... he sure is "off"! (*Taps finger on head. Curtain*)

*   *   *   *   *

SCENE 2

BEFORE RISE: NARRATOR *enters in front of curtain.*

NARRATOR: Scene 1 is over. We have seen the scene, set the set, and characterized the characters. Continuing with the same theatrical flourish your artistic tastes have come to demand, Scene 2 will star the stars, and plot the plot to a concluding conclusion. Will Aladdin find the Magic Lamp? Will he find riches and happiness? Or will he strike oil and live happily ever after? On with the story! (NARRATOR *exits as curtain opens.*)

TIME: *Half an hour later.*

SETTING: *Cave, with stone walls, cobwebs and dust. Door is in one wall. Trunks and boxes are scattered about. Shelves hold jars and vases. Carpets hang on walls.* JEANIE *is concealed inside large trunk. Another box holds lamps.*

AT RISE: *Stage is empty, except for* JEANIE *in box.*

HASSAN (*Offstage*): But the opening is too small. I can't get through that!

ALADDIN (*Offstage*): I know! That's why you needed me, remember? I'm supposed to wiggle through (*Entering as though crawling through small opening*) and get the Magic Lamp. (*Stands*) I'm in — and what do you know? Here's a door! (*Opens door*) Come on in.

HASSAN (*Entering*): All right, now what's all this about a Magic Lamp?

MAGIC LAMP (*Entering with a flourish, wearing black coat, like magician, and carrying wand and towels*): Ta-daaaaa! You want a Magic Lamp, you get a Magic Lamp! For my first bit of magic, I will take this ordinary paper towel (*Holds up towel for audience to see while keeping another towel rolled up in palm of hand*) and tear it into shreds. (*He does this as dialog continues*)

HASSAN: *This* is a Magic Lamp?

ALADDIN: Well, it's not exactly what I had in mind.

MAGIC LAMP (*Continuing to tear paper*): Have a little patience, please! I'm just beginning my act.

HASSAN (*To* ALADDIN): I thought you meant a magic *lamp* . . . one that grants wishes.

MAGIC LAMP: You expected Houdini? Give me a chance, will you? I haven't even finished my first trick yet. Now, I take all this shredded paper and roll it into a ball . . . a tiny, teensy ball. (*Does so as he speaks*) Then I pass my magic wand over it (*Does so*), say the magic word, abracadabra, and *PRESTO!* (*Exchanges shredded paper towel in hand with unshredded one concealed between thumb and palm*) We have an unshredded paper towel. (*Unfolds towel*) There, isn't that magic?

ALADDIN: I've seen that towel test on TV. They could use you for a commercial. But I was expecting something different from a Magic Lamp.

MAGIC LAMP (*Offended*): What? You have to be the most difficult audience since the Rocking Chair Quartet from the Over-80's Club substituted for the Golden Banana Rock Band. How about this? (*Pulls out string of scarves, concealed in sleeve or pocket*) Surely you will call this magic?

HASSAN: Say, I'm beginning to like this! In fact, I see some great sales possibilities here!

ALADDIN: But according to the story, that's not a Magic Lamp.

MAGIC LAMP: Critics! Always critics! How about this? A rabbit out of a hat. (*Takes off hat and pulls out what appears to be nothing*)

ALADDIN (*Looks closely*): I don't see a rabbit.

MAGIC LAMP: Well, it's not exactly a rabbit. It's more of a hair. Hair — get it? Hair? (*Laughs*) I think all really great people in magic should have a sense of humor, don't you?

HASSAN (*Chuckling*): Yes! I like it very much!

MAGIC LAMP: Good, then for you I shall do my most

mystifying feat of magic. I shall —

ALADDIN: Is that the only magic you do?

MAGIC LAMP: Hey, what's with you? You've got to be even worse than the audience when I followed Don Rickles at the "Speak Nice to Your Mother-in-Law Convention" — in Death Valley ... on Friday the thirteenth.

ALADDIN: Oh, it's not that I don't like your magic. It's good! It's just that I was expecting a magic *lamp* ... you know, with a genie.

MAGIC LAMP: Oh, you want to see Jeanie, my assistant. Why didn't you say so? This is one of my best bits of magic. Watch closely. I clap three times (*Does so*) ... and pass my wand over this trunk. (*Does so over trunk concealing* JEANIE) Ta-daaaaaa! Presto-appearo! (JEANIE *pops out of trunk and curtsies as* MAGIC LAMP *bows in exaggerated fashion.* JEANIE *does not speak, but audience should recognize by her miming that she is attracted to* ALADDIN. *She looks only at him and stands close to him.* ALADDIN *does not notice this.*)

HASSAN: Bravo! (*Applauding*) Bravo! You are terrific! Allow me to introduce myself. I am Hassan (*Offers business card*), biggest carpet dealer in all of Arabia.

ALADDIN: Carpets? You told me you were a predictor!

HASSAN: Yes, I am! I can predict a sale even before the customer knows it.

ALADDIN: But you said you could see all, hear all, know all.

HASSAN: Oh, that's just a sales gimmick to get inside houses so I can sell carpets. However, right now I truly *can* see all, hear all, know all, and I predict that we (*Indicates* MAGIC LAMP *and himself*) could team up and make a fortune!

MAGIC LAMP: A team? Who would get top billing?

HASSAN: *You* can have *total* billing. Here's how it would work: You would attract a crowd with your magic, then I would jump in with a sales pitch and sell my carpets. Sort of a "Magic Carpet" deal. What do you say?

MAGIC LAMP: Magic Carpet? I like it! When do we start?

HASSAN: Just as soon as you can pack your bag of tricks. By the way, can you make an elephant disappear?

MAGIC LAMP: An elephant disappear? Sure, that's easy. (*Gestures in mystic way, as* JEANIE *strikes various poses appropriate to magician's assistant, all the while keeping her eyes on* ALADDIN) Elephantus — begonus! (*Turns to look at* HASSAN) Well?

HASSAN: Well what?

MAGIC LAMP: Did you like it?

HASSAN: Did I like what?

MAGIC LAMP: The elephants.

HASSAN: What elephants? I don't see any elephants!

MAGIC LAMP: Of course not. You asked me to make them disappear!

HASSAN (*Chuckling, then laughing heartily*): Oh, we're going to sell lots and lots of carpets. (*Exits with* MAGIC LAMP)

ALADDIN: Hey! What about me? We were supposed to find a Magic Lamp . . . I mean, a lamp that is *magic*

... I mean — (*Shrugs and sits dejectedly down center*) I always thought this stery had a happy ending. (*During* ALADDIN's *speech* JEANIE *reaches into box upstage and pulls out lamp. She taps his shoulder and hands it to him.*) Oh, it's you. I suppose you want to sell me a lamp.

JEANIE (*Shakes head "no" and mimes that he should close eyes and rub lamp*)

ALADDIN (*Taking lamp*): Rub the lamp? It's worth a try. (*Closes eyes and rubs lamp*) I wish I had bags of gold. (*Nothing happens, so he tosses it aside.* JEANIE *gets another lamp and hands it to* ALADDIN.) Another? What have I got to lose? (*Closes eyes and rubs*) I wish I had boxes of diamonds. (*Nothing happens. He tosses lamp aside and takes a third from* JEANIE.) I wish I had stacks of silver. (*Repeats process with another lamp, speaking faster*) I wish I had pouches of rubies. (*Repeats, faster*) I wish I had strings of pearls. (*Quickly goes through several lamps one after another*) Satin robes ... Frankincense ... Oil paintings ... Palaces ... (*Stops, resting chin in hand dejectedly. He has one last lamp still in hand.*) I wish I knew which one was magic.

MOTHER (*Entering, looking bewildered*): I don't know how I got here, but you'd better come home quickly. The place is filling up with bags of gold and boxes of diamonds and stacks of silver and pouches of rubies, and —

ALADDIN: Bags of gold? (*Finds and picks up first discarded lamp*) Boxes of diamonds? (*Finds second discarded lamp*) Stacks of silver? (*Picks up third lamp*) Pouches of rubies? (*Begins picking up all lamps*) This is the kind of ending everyone wishes for.

MOTHER: That's my boy! I knew all along you could do it. All you needed was a woman's help. (*Shakes hands with* JEANIE)

ALADDIN (*Protesting*): Ah-h-h, Mom! (*Curtain*)

THE END

Sherwood Forest Revisited

New adventures of Robin Hood

Characters

NARRATOR
KING
SHERIFF OF ROTTINGHAM
ROBIN HOOD
MARIAN, *the King's daughter*
MERRY MEN, *extras*

SCENE 1

BEFORE RISE: NARRATOR *enters in front of curtain.*

NARRATOR: The story you are about to see is true. That is, it's a true account of a legend. Of course, it is true that legends cannot be verified — and it's also true that legends are sometimes invented to explain unknown events. But, generally speaking, they are supposed to be at least some of the time, partially, based on a little truth. Anyway, in this story, all the parts that are not true have very little to do with the true story anyway. This is the tale of the Great

Humanitarian Hero, the Renowned Gentleman Thief, the Immortal Master Bandit, and all-around Hey-nonny-nonny Guy: Robin Hood! So, without further truths, let our story begin. (*Exits. Curtains open.*)

TIME: *Long ago.*
SETTING: *King's throne room. Shields, swords, etc., hang on walls and there is a throne at center with bell rope hanging beside it.*
AT RISE: *The room is empty. Then* KING *enters with bag of money and sits on throne.*

KING: Suffering serfs, am I ever tired! It's been such a taxing day! Taxing knights, taxing damsels, taxing dragons. My subjects just don't realize how hard it is to think up all these new ways to collect taxes! (*Shifts position*) I need to get away and relax for several weeks and think of nothing. Too bad television hasn't been invented yet. Oh, well (*Pulls bell rope*), I can ring for the Jester and maybe have a few laughs. (ROBIN HOOD, *disguised as jester, enters, his head bowed, so the* KING *does not see his face.*)
ROBIN: You rang, Sire?
KING: Yes, Jester, amuse me with some of your traveling squire jokes. (*Suddenly*) Wait! (*Stands*) You're not the Jester — you're —
ROBIN (*Flinging off disguise, drawing sword and brandishing it with large sweeps*):
Yes! Hey nonny-nonny, 'tis I, Robin Hood.

Here is my decree:
Ask not what your country can do for you,
But what you can give to me.

KING: You! Robin Hood! You dare to enter my castle? (*Composing himself*) Obviously you have forgotten about my guards. (*Mocking laugh*) Ha, ha, ha — at last Robin Hood has made a mistake!

ROBIN:

Alack, you are right,
A mistake has been made.
But, whose has it been?
Will you wager this blade?

(*Holds sword next to* KING's *throat*)

KING: You fool! I'll wager nothing! All I have to do is pull on this (*Pulls bell rope*) — and my guards will be upon you before you can spout another "hey nonny-nonny!" (KING *smiles broadly. His expression begins to change as there is a long pause and no one comes.* KING *clears throat nervously.*)

ROBIN (*Folding arms nonchalantly*): Hey nonny-nonny ...

KING (*Getting more nervous*): Just one pull (*Pulls again*) on this bell rope, and the Sheriff of Rottingham will arrive in full armor before you can say, "Stand and deliver!"

ROBIN (*Smiling*):

Stand and deliver,
O generous giver.

KING (*Pulling rope frantically*): I'm the King! You can't rob me in my own castle! It's ... it's against the law!

ROBIN (*Stepping next to* KING):
> The poor will rejoice —
> For the King has no choice!

(*Holds out hand for money bag, which* KING *gives him*)

KING: I've heard of giving at the office, but this is ridiculous!

ROBIN (*Holding sword above head*):
> Hey nonny-nonny, a title I forswore,
> To rob from the rich and give to the poor!

(*Exits with flourish*)

KING (*Pulling rope vigorously*): Where are my guards? Modern technology — bah! (*Stops pulling cord*) I'll take old-fashioned lung power any day. (*Bellows*) Guards! (SHERIFF *enters. He speaks in manner of John Wayne and wears black patch over one eye.*)

SHERIFF: Let's get these cannons in a circle. Robin Hood is a-heading this way.

KING: You're too late, you silly sap. By this time Robin Hood is already heading that-a-way! (*Points toward exit*)

SHERIFF: Dad blast that varmint! I'd have had him with my fast draw if those little green Merry Men hadn't back-jumped me.

KING: Excuses! Excuses! That's all I hear! I want Robin Hood if you have to arrest every man in Sherwood Forest.

SHERIFF: We already did that! But Robin Hood escaped by dressing up like a woman.

KING: I want him if you have to burn down every tree in Sherwood Forest!

SHERIFF: We tried that, too, but those Merry Men of his picked up our flaming arrows and shot them right back at us. And oo — oh — did that ever smart!

KING (*Sitting*): Then what must we do to rid the kingdom of this pest?

SHERIFF: The way I got it figured, all we got to do is make the poor folks rich — then Robin Hood won't need to rob from the rich and give to the poor.

KING (*With disgust*): With guys like you on my side, how did I ever get to be King?

SHERIFF: Don't worry, Cap'n. I aim to put Robin Hood behind bars if it's the last thing I do.

KING: Let's rephrase that: if you do *not* put him behind bars, it *will* be the last thing you do! Now get out there and get to work on it!

SHERIFF: Yes, Cap'n. (*Starts to exit*)

KING: And stop calling me "Cap'n." It's Sire or Your Majesty!

SHERIFF (*Moving back to* KING *and bowing*): Yes, Cap'n Sire, Your Majesty. (*Again starts toward exit*)

KING (*Standing*): Wait! (SHERIFF *moves back as* KING *paces.*) There may be a better way to silence that "hey nonny-nonny." Send in my daughter, Princess Marian.

SHERIFF: Yes, Cap'n. (*Hurries out*)

KING (*Calling after him*): And don't call me Cap'n! (*Returns to throne and sits*) An idiot sheriff, a brazen thief. If it weren't for the knighthood rebates, the dragon-lobby kickbacks, and the Holy Grail graft, being King would hardly be worthwhile.

MARIAN (*Entering*): Hi, Dad. You wanted to see me hear.

KING: Ah-h-h-h! Princess Marian — heir to my throne, bearer of my noble lineage, harbinger of the heritage — you have come.

MARIAN: Sure. So what's happening in Thronesville today?

KING: It's that pretentious poacher! He invaded the sanctity of my castle! He infringed upon the privacy of my noble person!

MARIAN: Who did what?

KING: Robin Hood! He was here; he took my money!

MARIAN: Robin Hood was here in the castle? Like *wow,* Pops! He's really a gutsy guy!

KING: Yes — he was here — spouting that rabble-rallying cry, "Rob from the rich and give to the poor!"

MARIAN: Neat-o! That guy in green really knows how to get it all together. So why rap with me?

KING: I want you to go into Sherwood Forest, pretend to be poor, and join Robin Hood's band. Then, you shall supply me with all his secret plans, and tell me the location of his hideout, so we can catch the Robbing Rogue.

MARIAN: Like *wow*! It will be sort of a medieval CIA! (*Moves to exit*) Sure, Pops, I can dig it. (*Exits*)

KING: Good, but don't call me "Pops." Call me ... call me ... (*To audience*) Just call me when you have the goods on Robin Hood. (*Curtain*)

* * * * *

SCENE 2

BEFORE RISE: NARRATOR *enters in front of curtain.*

NARRATOR: Before we return to the play and continue with the mythological plot of the mythical Robin Hood, let us reiterate the story — just in case you *mythed* it. One, Robin Hood robbed the King; two, the King wants his money back, plus Robin Hood; three, the Sheriff cannot catch Robin Hood; so, four, the King has sent his daughter, Princess Marian, to spy on him. Even Shakespeare would have difficulty sorting the intricacies of this interwoven plot. What will happen? Let Scene Two begin. (NARRATOR *exits. Curtains open.*)

SETTING: *Sherwood Forest.*

AT RISE: *The stage is empty. Then* MARIAN *enters, dressed as a peasant.*

MARIAN: Hey, where have I been all my life? Sherwood Forest is right on! I really groove on this outdoors stuff. (*Looks around happily*)

ROBIN (*Entering with flourish, carrying money bag taken from* KING):
> Hey nonny-nonny, 'tis I, Robin Hood.
> Sherwood Forest is my neighborhood.

MARIAN: Well, hi there to you, too!

ROBIN:
> I seek not your "hi's," nor your "heys," nor your "ho's,"
> Your coins I'll take this day.

> I rob from the rich and give to the poor,
> Then I go on my way.

MARIAN: In that case, hold on! I'm not rich. I'm just (*Sweetly*) a poor little girl who's lost and alone in the forest.

ROBIN:

> Poor? Didst thou say poor?
> Well, hey nonny-nonny, speaketh no more;
> I rob from the rich and give to the poor!

(*Hands her the money bag*)

MARIAN: For me? But I didn't mean "poor," like, no money, I meant "poor," like —

ROBIN (*Brandishing sword*):

> Hey nonny-nonny and now I must go.
> The world is at my call.
> I pledge allegiance to the poor
> With freedom and justice for all!

(*Exits*)

MARIAN (*Calling after him*): Hey, but I . . . (*Turns and moves down center*) Would you believe that? He actually gave me money! He thought I was poor and he gave me money! Robin Hood is right on!

KING (*Entering with* SHERIFF): Ah, Marian! There you are. What secrets have you wheedled from that Pesky Pilferer that will enable us to entrap him?

SHERIFF: Why don't we just put the archers in a circle . . . .

KING: Quiet! (*To* MARIAN) Well?

MARIAN: He's straight, Dad. He really does rob the rich and give to the poor. Look! (*Holds up money bag*)

KING: That's my money!

MARIAN: I said I was poor and he gave it to me — just like that!

KING: Hm-m-m . . . an honest thief. Now that complicates things.

SHERIFF: Just get him and all his men to ride toward me, and I'll put the reins in my mouth, grab my six-guns, and head straight toward them, firing.

KING: You bungling boob! Guns haven't been invented yet.

SHERIFF: They haven't?

KING: No!

SHERIFF: Then no wonder I haven't caught Robin Hood yet!

KING (*To audience*): I'm going to put a tax on hiring relatives. The Queen will owe me a fortune. Oh, well, at least we got my money back. We'll catch Robin Hood another time. (*To* SHERIFF) Get the money and we'll start home. (*Starts to exit.* SHERIFF *goes to* MARIAN, *who clutches bag of money.*)

MARIAN: Oh, no, you don't! Robin Hood gave it to me and I'm going to keep it!

KING: Don't be ridiculous! It's my money. It still has my royal seal on it. (*To* SHERIFF) Take it and let's go.

MARIAN: Over my dead body!

SHERIFF: All right, let's get the guards in a circle!

KING: Now wait a minute. She is not an enemy of the Crown! She is my daughter, the Royal Princess. Just take the money. (*Reaches for it*)

MARIAN: Touch me and I'll scream! (KING *hesitates, then reaches for money again.*) Help! Hey nonny-

nonny! Help! (ROBIN HOOD *enters with drawn sword, followed by* MERRY MEN, *dressed in green.*)

ROBIN:
>Hey nonny-nonny,
>A damsel doth squeal!
>Stand down, you foul knaves,
>Or my blade you will feel!

MARIAN: Robin Hood, these guys are trying to rip off all the money you gave me!

ROBIN:
>Gadzooks and for shame!
>Such a sinister deed!
>Two against one
>Is a scoundrel's ill creed.

KING: But, good sir, I am just a poor king, while this girl has all that money — see?

ROBIN (*To* MARIAN):
>I say, good woman, can this be true?
>Does all that money belong to you?

MARIAN: Yes! I'm ... I'm rich!

ROBIN:
>Well, hey nonny-nonny, alas and alack!
>I rob from the rich, so give me your sack!

(*Takes money bag and gives it to* KING; MERRY MEN *exit.*)

MARIAN: Oh-oh! Did I ever goof on word choice that time!

KING (*To* ROBIN): Thank you, kind sir. You are a true gentleman of your chosen profession.

SHERIFF: Is it time to get the coachmen in a circle?

KING: No, you ignoble idiot, it's time to get out! (*Exits with* SHERIFF)

ROBIN (*Flourishing sword*):

>Hey nonny-nonny and now I must go,
>
>My country 'tis of thee.
>
>I rob from the rich and give to the poor;
>
>O say can the dawn's light you see?

(*Starts to exit*)

MARIAN: Now just hold on a minute, man. You're not the brainiest guy I ever met, but I really dig your dedication. How about the two of us tying the "I do" knot, then spending the happily-ever-after grooving in this greenery?

ROBIN:

>Well, hey nonny-nonny. Sound drums and a fife!
>
>Dost thou wish to be Maid Marian, my wife?

MARIAN: Well, I had *Ms.* Hood in mind, but if you promise you won't invite those little green Merry Men to dinner more than once a month, I'll O.K. it for the Maid Marian bit. (*Exits arm-in-arm with* ROBIN.)

KING (*Entering with* SHERIFF): Things do have a way of working out, don't they? This sure beats collecting taxes!

SHERIFF: You mean after all this I don't get to slap Robin Hood behind bars and collect the ree-ward?

KING: No. I have just solved three of my biggest problems! One, my daughter will get married and move out of the castle; and two, any time I need money I'll

just send you out here disguised to look poor, and
Robin Hood will give it to you.

SHERIFF (*Counting on fingers*): But I thought you said
you had solved *three* problems.

KING: Yes! I did! *You* are going to be spending a lot of
time out here looking poor! (*Curtain*)

THE END

The Sorcerer's Apprentice Finds a Helping Hand

Don't practice magic without a license

Characters

NARRATOR
SORCERER
WIFE
HAND
WITCH
GOOD FAIRY
PAPERBOY
SALESMAN

BEFORE RISE: NARRATOR *enters in front of curtain.*

NARRATOR: This is the play about the Sorcerer's Apprentice. In case you've forgotten, the Sorcerer's Apprentice is the story of a magician who is getting old. "Old," in case you've forgotten, is what everybody wants to be until they get there—then they don't want to be anymore. Anyway, the Sorcerer decides he needs to take on an apprentice to help him with his feats of magic. An apprentice, in case you've forgotten, is the old way they used to have to get kids to work for nothing. Nowadays they call it "getting an allowance." In this story, the apprentice just doesn't, somehow, seem to work out too well and the Sorcerer has to find another solution. To find out what this is, let's get on with the story, lest we forget. We see that it opens . . . (*Curtain opens*) with the Sorcerer hard at work perfecting his great supernatural powers. (*Exits.*)

SETTING: *The Sorcerer's laboratory, with cluttered table holding vials and beakers with tubes running from one to another. On one side are tall writing desk and stool. Nearby is a large box concealing person who plays the Hand. Box has large book on top of it.*

AT RISE: SORCERER, *with long, gray beard, is seated at desk. He is dozing, chin in hand. His head nods, falling off his hand. He switches hands and continues to snore.*

WIFE (*Entering*): So this is what you call "working late at the office." (SORCERER *wakes with a start at sound of voice and pretends to be working. He moves and speaks very slowly simulating old person.*)

SORCERER: I was just working on some new Magical Incantations to unlock the secrets of the Universe.

WIFE: Magical Incantations — ha! You're getting so old and lazy the only "Magical Incantation" you can manage is to persuade the sorcerers' union to keep

you on the payroll. Look at this place! It's a mess —
and all you ever do is sit on that stool and sleep.
(SORCERER *nods, as if falling off to sleep.*) Now pay
attention! (WIFE *nudges* SORCERER) I came down
here to check on the sunshine I need for this afternoon's Royal Auxiliary Picnic. The Queen has named
me chairperson and I want to impress her that, after
all, I *am* the Sorcerer's Wife (*Looks at him dozing*)
... for whatever that's worth. (*Moves close and
speaks into his ear*) Sunshine ... for the picnic ...
this afternoon. Got that?

SORCERER: Oh, is this the day you wanted sunshine
for the picnic? (*Takes pencil, slowly touches point to
tongue, then reaches up and marks another day off
calendar which hangs above desk*)

WIFE (*Exasperated*): And get me something for a headache, too. (SORCERER *picks up wand and slowly
moves to box concealing* HAND. *He leafs through
large book on top, nods head, then taps box with
hand and chants.*)

SORCERER:
O mystic powers that be,
Send a headache remedy. (HAND *rises slowly
out of top of box, holding tongue depressor.* SOR-
CERER *takes it, then* HAND *moves slowly back into
box.* SORCERER *gives tongue depressor to* WIFE.)
Here, this should do it.

WIFE: This is a tongue depressor. How is that supposed to stop my headache?

SORCERER (*Taking it back*): Oh, *your* headache. I
thought you meant something for *my* headache.

(*Aside*) A tongue depressor won't do. She needs a real gag to keep her quiet and cure my headache.

WIFE (*Starting toward exit*): My mother warned me about marrying a sorcerer who thought he was funny, but would I listen? (*Pauses at exit*) Just don't forget the picnic. I want you to be there on time. (*Starts to exit, then returns*) And don't forget to change into your new robe. (*Again exits and returns*) The one with the stars on it. (*Exits and returns*) And wear your good hat! (*Exits and returns*) And sunshine ... remember I want sunshine! (*Exits*)

SORCERER: Picnics ... I'm getting too old for picnics. (*Moves to* HAND, *looks up something in large book, taps box with wand and chants.*)

> Let there be sunshine all the day through;
> But let a little rain fall, too. (HAND *rises out of box, indicates "O.K." by making a circle with thumb and forefinger, then slowly goes back into box.*)

WITCH (*Entering on broom and running about stage; with cackling laughter*): I come to wreak havoc and bring misery into your life. (*Cackles*)

SORCERER (*Unperturbed*): You're too late. I'm already married.

WITCH (*Continuing to scurry about*): I'm here to cast an evil spell on all humanity. (*Makes bewitching motions as* SORCERER *nods off to sleep. She nudges him.*) Come on! Wake up so I can put you to sleep!

SORCERER: Quit flying around and tell me why you're really here. (WITCH *stops and leans on table to catch breath*)

WITCH: Oh, all right. I'm getting too old for all this "witchcraft" business anyway ... And you are, too! I'm a dissatisfied customer. I have a consumer complaint. That last apple you sold me didn't cast the right spell. I used it on some fink prince, and instead of turning into a frog, he only said "ribet" and gave everybody warts. Things like that could ruin my reputation.

SORCERER: Do you want a refund?

WITCH: No, what I really want is to chuck the whole works, cauldron and all, and let the new rookie witches have it. Then I could just ride my broom off into the moonset.

SORCERER: Not me. I'd rather stay at work. Otherwise I'd have nothing to do but sit at home all day.

WITCH: What's wrong with that?

SORCERER: With *my* wife?

GOOD FAIRY (*From offstage; in sugary voice*): Yoo-hoo! Anybody home? It's me, the Good Fairy. I'm coming in. Do you have all your bats locked up? You know how I hate to be around old bats. (*Enters*)

WITCH: If you're talking about me, I'll clobber you!

GOOD FAIRY: Oh, goodness, no. I could never mean you, Wicked Witch of the West. I mean those awful mice-like creatures with wings. (*Shivers at thought*) Oh!

WITCH (*Moving toward* GOOD FAIRY, *mockingly*): I like those fanged, furry, flying creatures ... and I like snakes that slither and crawl, and spiders ...

GOOD FAIRY: Please! You know I don't like to hear

about those dreadful things. I'm the Good Fairy.

SORCERER: Stop, you two. Can't a man get any rest in his own domicile?

GOOD FAIRY: It's all her fault. She always likes to stir things up.

WITCH (*Cackling and pretending to stir a cauldron*): "Bubble, bubble, toil and trouble." That's what witches are for, my dear. Trouble. And we don't like Good Fairies who go around and undo all our evil works. So, state your business and then get out.

GOOD FAIRY: I came to tell the Sorcerer that the wand dust he sold me last week must have been stale. (*Waves wand and gold sprinkles float down.* NOTE: *Gold may be gold powdered tempera held in hand or in wand, which is uncapped before being waved.*) Poor Cinderella was dancing at the Grand Ball and started changing back at 11:30 instead of midnight.

WITCH: Ha! I'd like to have been there to see her stranded at the Palace gate with six white mice and a pumpkin. (SORCERER *moves to table and slowly pours solutions from beaker to beaker, vial to vial, then leans against table and dozes.*)

GOOD FAIRY: Sir? (*Nudges him*) Mr. Sorcerer?

SORCERER (*Awakening*): Yes, what can I do for you?

GOOD FAIRY: The wand dust? You were mixing a new batch for me.

SORCERER: Oh, yes, wand dust. (*Holds beaker up to check color, puts in cork and hands it to* GOOD FAIRY) Here, this should do it.

GOOD FAIRY: Thank you. (*Takes beaker*) O Great

Sorcerer, I do not wish to appear rude or imperti-
nent, but is there any way I can help you? Now that
you are in your Golden Years, you don't seem to get
around as fast as you used to. Maybe you should ...
(SORCERER *is asleep so she nudges him.*) Maybe you
should hire an apprentice.

WITCH: Say, that's not a bad idea! A sorcerer's apprentice! That way he could carry on with all your great
incantations and secret formulas. (*To* GOOD FAIRY)
You really are a Good Fairy.

GOOD FAIRY: Well, I try. (*Moves to exit*) Toodleloo,
everybody, until next time. (*Exits*)

WITCH (*Moving toward exit, talking to self*): I should
get an apprentice, too. Someone to help me fly
my broom. But, who could I get? Not just anybody
can make a good mean witch. (*Exits*)

SORCERER: How about my wife? She has practice!

WIFE (*Entering*): What are you yelling about me, your
wife, and practice?

SORCERER: Nothing. What I said was "life"... I said
I had spent my entire life practicing the, ah ...
secrets of the Orient.

WIFE: Secrets of the Orient, Humph! The only secrets
of the Orient *you* know are found in Chinese fortune
cookies. Why aren't you changed for the picnic?

SORCERER (*Tapping box with wand*):
This is all I want to hear.
Make this woman disappear. (HAND *starts
out of box.*)

WIFE: If you don't stop mumbling and do as I say, I'm

going home to Mother. (HAND *disappears.*)

SORCERER (*Patting box*): Come back, come back! It still might work!

WIFE: Now, hurry up and get changed so we won't be late for the picnic.

SORCERER: But I can't leave now. I'm expecting the salesman from Sorcerer's Supply this afternoon. I'm getting low on bat wings and lizards' gizzards, and I'm completely out of warthog hairs and rodent tails.

WIFE: Make a list and tack it on the door. Just be there! And remember — *sunshine!* (*Exits*)

SORCERER: Maybe I do need an apprentice. That way I could take a few days off now and then — go fishing. What do you think? (*Taps* HAND *box.* HAND *rises slowly out of box holding fish.*) That's not what I mean, and you know it! (HAND *disappears back into box with fish. Knock on door is heard.*)

PAPERBOY (*Offstage*): Paperboy! (*Enters*) Collecting — you're $3.75 overdue.

SORCERER (*Reaching into pockets*): Bills, bills, bills. Here. (*Counts money into* PAPERBOY'*s hand*) One, two, two-fifty, two-sixty, two-seventy . . . seventy-five . . . (*Finishes searching in all pockets*) That's all.

PAPERBOY: You're a dollar short. (SORCERER *looks on table, desk, finally moves to box and taps.*)

SORCERER:
　　I need a dollar.
　　For the caller. (HAND *rises, holding dollar bill.* SORCERER *takes it and gives it to* PAPERBOY *as* HAND *disappears into box.*)

PAPERBOY: Hey, that's neat! (*Taps box*) How about a

repeat? (*Rhymes without realizing it.* HAND *rises with bill, then disappears back into box after* PAPER-BOY *takes it.*) Boy, this is great! How does a person ever get to be a sorcerer?

SORCERER: Well, it takes abounding knowledge (WIFE *enters and stands at entrance during his speech. She is wet and water is dripping from her umbrella. She scowls at* SORCERER *who is unaware of her presence*) ... comprehensive intellect, unbiased judgment, discriminating insight —

WIFE: Too bad it doesn't include "fast feet" because when I catch you — (*Brandishes umbrella*)

SORCERER: Now, wait just a minute. You clearly said you wanted sunshine. Look outside. Is the sun shining?

WIFE: Yes, the sun is shining, but there's also a *downpour!*

SORCERER: Did you say anything about rain? No! All you said was, "Make the sun shine." And the sun *is* shining.

WIFE: Then let me restate the request. Make the weather whatever you want. But ... you have five minutes to change and come out there beside me. (*Exits*)

SORCERER (*Tapping* HAND *box*):
    Rain, rain, go away.
    I can see it's not my day. (HAND *rises, snaps fingers, returns.*)

PAPERBOY: I'd sure like to know how to be a sorcerer.

SORCERER: My boy, it's not an easy business. There's a lot to learn, and it takes a long time. To become a sorcerer, one must first be an apprentice. (*Looks* PAPERBOY *over for a minute*) It just so happens that I'm looking for a fine young lad to be my apprentice, and to start this very afternoon. (*Takes off hat and places it on* PAPERBOY*'s head*)

PAPERBOY: Wow! Imagine that! Me, a sorcerer!

SORCERER: The first thing you must learn is to obey instructions. Never do anything without my instructions. And most of all, whatever you do, do not try to use the Helping Hand. It takes special training. You may get into trouble.

PAPERBOY: Whatever you say. You're the boss. Just tell me what to do, and I'll do it.

SORCERER: You may start by sweeping the floor. I'll be back in about an hour. (*Exits*)

PAPERBOY (*Prancing about, admiring self in hat*): Wait till the other paperboys see me! Just think, no more getting up early on snowy mornings and trudging off before breakfast to throw newspapers on somebody's roof. When I want something now, I'll just step here (*Goes to* HAND) and demand it. The Sorcerer told me not to do this, but I'm starving. It couldn't do any harm to ask for (*Loudly*) a big, juicy hamburger medium rare, hold the mustard, and a thick, chocolate milkshake. (*Nothing happens.*) I want a big hamburger and a chocolate milkshake. (*Nothing happens. He knocks on box.*) Hey, inside, can you hear me? I said I wanted a hamburger and a milkshake. (*Looks at sides of box*) What's wrong? Are you unplugged? Hello? Hello?

SALESMAN (*Entering with briefcase*): Hello to you.

Sorcerer's Supply calling. How are you fixed for dried spider legs? Or buzzard blood? (*Opens case*) How about a new apple poison? Guaranteed to last ninety-nine years or your money back — after ninety-nine years, that is. (*Looks closely at* PAPERBOY) Say, you're new here, aren't you?

PAPERBOY: I'm the Sorcerer's Apprentice.

SALESMAN: Well, then, you'll be interested in a magic wand. (*Takes one from case*) This one is the latest model. It's good for spells, incantations, conjuring, and general run-of-the-mill abracadabras.

PAPERBOY: Yeah! I like it! Can I charge it?

SALESMAN (*Putting it back into case and showing sign on side reading* CASH ONLY): Sorry, in God we trust — all others pay cash.

PAPERBOY: Oh . . . say! Maybe you can tell me how this works. (*Indicates box*) Then I can get some money.

SALESMAN: That's the Sorcerer's Helping Hand. The only thing I know about it is that it takes the Sorcerer to make it work.

PAPERBOY: I made it work earlier, but now it won't.

SALESMAN: Don't sweat it, kid. You're the Sorcerer's Apprentice. He'll show you all that stuff sooner or later, then you'll have plenty of money. Right now I'd better be on my way. I still have to call on a witch doctor today, and every time I keep him waiting I get sharp pains in my chest.

PAPERBOY: O.K. I guess I'd better (*Walks past* HAND *box and taps it in passing*) get a broom and clean the room. (HAND *rises with broom.* NOTE: *If box is too small for broom, it can be leaning close to box where* HAND *can reach it to hand to* PAPERBOY) Look! It's working! (*Takes broom as* HAND *returns to box. The minute broom is touched to floor it begins to "pull"* PAPERBOY *back and forth across room.*) This is easy! The broom is doing all the work! I'll have the floor swept in no time. (*Continues two or three times across floor, then stops*) There, all done. (*Broom continues to "pull" him and he can't let go.*) Stop! We're through. It's clean already! Help! It won't let go. (*Continues to be pulled across room*)

SALESMAN: What do you mean, it won't let go? (*Grabs broom, still carrying briefcase, and is pulled back and forth*) Oh, that's what you mean by "It won't let go."

PAPERBOY: What'll we do?

SALESMAN: Let's push it over to the Helping Hand.

PAPERBOY (*Tapping* HAND *box in passing*): Stop! Make the broom stop!

SALESMAN (*Speaking to* HAND *box*): Stop! Help! . . . Rhymes! That's it, rhymes! The Sorcerer always used rhymes to make it work! . . . ah . . . Don't sweep . . . ah, creep. (*Both take crouching position and are pulled slowly as though "creeping."*) No, no! Don't make *us* creep! (HAND *is out of box, snapping fingers*)

PAPERBOY: Try another rhyme. That one doesn't work right!

SALESMAN: All right. Stop . . . hop! (*Both begin hopping up and down.*) No! Not hop! Stop! (SORCERER *enters.*)

SORCERER: What's going on here? I told you not to use the Hand. (*Goes to box, pausing to take hat from* PAPERBOY)

SALESMAN: Hurry! I can't take much more of this! My lizard tongues will get smashed up with the unicorn horns! (SORCERER *opens book. Broom continues to pull* SALESMAN *and* PAPERBOY *around room.*)

PAPERBOY: I'm sorry I disobeyed your order — please make it stop.

SORCERER (*Tapping box*):
Time to stop,
Before they drop.

PAPERBOY (*Dropping broom and collapsing to knees*): Wow! That was terrible!

SALESMAN (*Leaning against table, exhausted and shaking briefcase*): Oh, listen to it! I just know everything's broken. (*Opens case*) Oh, no! Everything is all mixed together. Maybe I can sell it to the witch doctor as Strong Medicine. After all, it should either kill or cure. (*Closes case and moves to exit*) See you next week. (*Exits*)

PAPERBOY: You won't see me! I quit! Delivering papers is easier than this. (*Exits*)

SORCERER: Well, here I am, right back where I started. I'm still old, and getting older. Wait! I know what the answer is. (*Looks in book, smiles, taps box with wand*)
No more old and slow for me.
Make me young — say, twenty-three. (HAND *appears, holding cup, and splashes* SORCERER *with water. He straightens, jumps into air. He pulls off beard and throws off his robe, revealing T-shirt*

and blue jeans.) Ya-hoo! I feel like a teen-ager! I should have thought of this forty years ago!

WIFE (*Entering*): What's all this racket? Where's my husband?

SORCERER: He's gone — gone for good.

WIFE (*Going to box*): Gone my eye. I know you when I see you. And taking forty years off your life doesn't fool me. (*Picks up wand*) Two can play this game. (*Taps box*)

> Make me young and trim,
>
> Same as you just did for him. (HAND *rises with cup, splashes* WIFE *with water. She turns to* SORCERER.) See, there's enough in the Fountain of Youth for both of us. (*She pulls off veil with attached wig, revealing a young woman in blue jeans and sneakers.*) You're right! It feels great!

SORCERER: I think I'm going to enjoy this. (*Extends arm to* WIFE) Let's go on that picnic! (*Curtain*)

THE END

Production Notes

BIG, BAD WOLF AT THE DOOR

Characters: 4 male; 2 female; 1 male or female for Narrator.

Playing Time: 15 minutes.

Costumes: Red Riding Hood wears red cape with hood, dress; Narrator and Wolf wear regular street clothes. If desired, Wolf can wear animal mask of *papier-mâché* or a paper bag, and a tail, etc.; Father-in-Law, Junior and Big Al wear gangster-like dark suits with collars turned up, hats with brims down; Grandma wears long skirt, shawl, Granny glasses, hair in bun.

Properties: Picnic basket with several old 78 rpm records, blanket, thermometer, ice bag, notebook, large handkerchief.

Setting: Scene 1, a forest — this scene may be played before curtain. Scene 2, Grandma's living room — an easy chair, center, with a table beside it. There is a tablecloth on table which reaches to the floor. Lamps, pictures and other old-fashioned items complete the furnishings.

Lighting: No special effects.

JACK, THE BEANSTALK AND CHICKEN

Characters: 3 male; 2 female; 1 male or female.

Playing Time: 15 minutes.

Costumes: Jack and Mother, appropri-

ate fairy tale costumes; Narrator, modern, everyday dress; Chicken, feathers and simulated comb; W. C. Fieldston, tall hat, dress coat, gloves, cane; Giant, green tunic and tights, green pointed hat.

Properties: Large medicine bottle; hat; megaphone.

Setting: Scene 1, kitchen in Jack's cottage, a room with table, two chairs, a mirror, and a working window. Scene 2, Giant's Castle, a room with banner or tapestry hanging from stone wall, and a throne-like chair. Everything is standard size except for large nest in one corner.

Lighting: No special effects.

Sound: Slide whistle, as indicated in text.

THE TORTOISE AND THE HARE HIT THE ROAD

Characters: 9 male or female.

Playing Time: 20 minutes.

Costumes: Appropriate animal costumes, with makeup, false ears, tails, etc., and masks, or everyday clothes, with a sign around each actor's neck, reading FOX and so forth. Bear also has "Smokey the Bear" ranger's hat. Narrator is in everyday clothes.

Properties: Sign reading ONLY YOU CAN PREVENT FOREST FIRES; purse and umbrella for Chicken; play money.

Setting: A forest scene, with stump at

center. For Scene 2, stump is removed, and a sign is at center (high-jump standard may also be used), with START on one side and FINISH on the other. There is a throne, or kingly chair, at one side.
Lighting: No special effects.

MEET DR. FRANKENSTEIN

Characters: 5 male; 3 female; 1 male or female for Tombstone; as many extras as desired for Other Children.
Playing Time: 15 minutes.
Costumes: Dr. Frankenstein, black suit, coat, gloves. Igor, baggy pants, sweatshirt covering "hump" on one shoulder, gloves. Wolfman, ordinary clothes, but with hair on face and hands. Dracula, green cape, suit, white face, slick, shiny hair with widow's peak. Tombstone, a box shaped like a tombstone and painted gray, worn over head and arms and extending to knees, with RIP lettered on front. Vampira, long, slinky black dress, exaggerated makeup, long black hair. Happy Medium, long, baggy skirt, shawl, gypsy scarf on head. Boy, Girl and Children wear raincoats and everyday dress.
Properties: Crystal ball, pocket watch.
Setting: A room in a haunted house, with a window upstage, and a door at one side. There is a coat tree near door. Furniture is covered with sheets. Fireplace may be in an upstage wall, if desired.
Lighting: Dim throughout; lightning, as indicated in text.
Sound: Creaking door, wind, thunder, throughout. Actor playing Tombstone can hold a microphone inside costume to give added volume to voice. Speaker for microphone may be concealed onstage.

CURSES! FOILED AGAIN!

Characters: 1 female; 3 male; 2 male or female for Narrators; as many female as desired for Ladies.
Playing Time: 15 minutes.
Costumes: Nell wears long frilly dress with bows, lace and ribbons; Bruce wears boots, stocking cap, plaid shirt and jeans; Nasty wears black cape, pants, shirt, boots and has slicked hair and a moustache; Oliver wears western outfit; Ladies wear long dresses, shawls, etc. Narrators may wear period costumes.
Properties: Handcuffs; ax, which may be cardboard; tree branches.
Setting: There is a backdrop showing a residential small town, with picket fence, steeple, and many trees. Backdrop is removed for Scene 2. Two podiums are downstage right and left. A piano is on or in front of stage.
Lighting: No special effects.
Sound: Piano, as indicated in text.

CINDERELLA FINDS TIME

Characters: 5 male; 5 female.
Playing Time: 15 minutes.
Costumes: Traditional fairy tale costumes. Narrator wears modern street clothes. For Clock, a clock face is painted on a large carton (with armholes and eyeholes) which covers the actor's head and shoulders.
Properties: Wand, scroll, box containing many pairs of shoes.
Setting: The kitchen in the Stepmother's house. There are a table, two chairs, and a fireplace. In one wall is a window which opens and closes.
Lighting: No special effects.

THE WAY-OUT WIZARD OF OZ

Characters: 1 male; 3 female; 2 male or

female for Wizard and Scarecrow; one extra can work offstage noises.
Playing Time: 12 to 15 minutes.
Costumes: Dorothy wears old-fashioned, long dress with bow in hair, and changes into silver tennis shoes. Scarecrow has patched trousers and coat with straw protruding at sleeves and legs, flannel shirt, straw hat. Plasticman wears an outfit resembling a white plastic bleach jug, hat in shape of bottle, with bottle cap, made of cardboard and *papier-mâché,* painted white. Lioness wears tan body stocking, has pointed ears, tail, and whiskers. She carries whistle around neck. Wizard has long, bright robe patched with sorcerer's moons and stars, mystic-looking crown, and broken wand (in pocket). Witch has gray, scraggly hair, wears black gown, tall, pointed hat, and can carry broom.
Properties: Silver tennis shoes; whistle; broken wand; grooming kit with comb, mirror, nail file, etc.; electric power cell (can be made of cardboard and resemble oversized battery); gold medal; trophy; airline flight bag and ticket.
Setting: Forest, with exotic palms and fronds of various striped and polka-dotted colors, sky, clouds, grass, etc., all of unusual colors and shapes. A few cornstalks surround Scarecrow.
Lighting: No special effects unless dimming is used when chimes sound.
Special Effects: Fan creates blowing wind at Dorothy's entrance. Every time Wizard "wishes," chimes should sound offstage and items can simply be tossed onstage immediately following sound. If desired, special flashpot creating puff of smoke can be used onstage to indicate "magic." Items "appear" during smoke. Wind-up

noise can be made by any cranking instrument (party noisemaker works well).

PTA TRIUMPHS AGAIN

Characters: 2 male; 2 female; 3 male or female for Announcer, and Sign Holders.
Playing Time: 10 minutes.
Costumes: PTA Mom wears long dress, wire-rimmed glasses, and shawl. Her hair is in bun. Darling Nell wears frilly dress and has bow in hair. She is made up with rosy cheeks and long lashes. Villain wears traditional black cape, top hat, moustache, etc. Hero is in suit and bow tie. He has slicked-down hair. NOTE: If desired, school principal may take part of Hero.
Properties: Knitting basket and needles; hanky; two signs (one with HISS on one side and HOORAY! on reverse, second reading BOO and APPLAUSE on reverse).
Setting: PTA Mom's living room, decorated with old-fashioned furnishings, including rocking chair, floor lamp, old family photos or daguerreotypes, large sampler reading GOD BLESS THE PTA on wall, etc.
Sound: If possible, there should be a pianist in the orchestra pit to play a few bars of appropriate music for entrances and at other points throughout play, as indicated in text. Recorded music may also be used.

PINOCCHIO IN EQUAL OPPORTUNITY LAND

Characters: 3 male; 2 female; 1 male or male for Narrator.
Playing Time: 15 minutes.
Costumes: Geppetto, regular clothes with apron, full moustache. Pinoc-

chio, short brightly-colored trousers with suspenders, strings attached to wrists and ankles, long pointed false nose in pocket. Shirley, frilly skirt and blouse with lace, worn over rolled-up jeans and sweater; hat in jeans pocket. Fairy Modmother, current far-out clothing. Customer, cane, spectacles, gray hair, etc. Narrator, regular school clothes.
Properties: Wand decorated with flowers.
Setting: Cluttered, messy toy shop. There is workbench downstage, with an easy chair nearby. Shelves left, right, and rear should be overcrowded with wagons, drums, dolls, stuffed animals, soldiers, hobby horses, etc.
Sound: Triangle for offstage bell sound.

GOOD AS GOLDILOCKS

Characters: 3 male; 2 female; 1 male or female for Narrator.
Playing Time: 15 minutes.
Costumes: Bears wear suits of rough brown material and half-masks of papier-mâché, to look like bears. Uncle Groucho wears business suit, oversized eyebrows, and moustache. He has dark-rimmed glasses. Goldilocks has long blond hair and wears frilly dress.
Properties: Fake cigar, 3 bowls — one large, one small, one medium, napkins, silverware, large kettle, large wooden spoon.
Setting: Kitchen in home of Three Bears. Table is at center, with three chairs around it — large, medium, and small. Simulated fireplace with a hook on which to hang kettle is on rear wall. Samplers and pictures hang on walls; there is a window on one wall. Exits lead to other rooms, and outside.
Lighting: No special effects.

LET'S HEAR IT FOR THE PIED PIPER!

Characters: 2 male; 1 female; 3 male or female for Councilors.
Playing Time: 15-20 minutes.
Costumes: Lord Mayor and Councilors wear long, ornate robes, with pendants. Lord Mayor has double-crowned hat. Christina wears long, colorful dress of period. Piper carries kazoo, wears multi-colored body suit with cape, troubadour hat with large feather, and beads.
Properties: Kazoo; oversized book that can have a page torn out; quill pen; coins representing guilders.
Setting: Council Room in Town Hall of Hamlin. Exit on one side, large window opposite. Long table is center with at least three chairs. Crests, other royal adornments are on wall. Safe is in corner.
Lighting: No special effects.

SLEEPING BEAUTY WAKES UP

Characters: 3 male; 1 female; 3 male or female for Rebel and Guards.
Playing Time: 20 minutes.
Costumes: King wears small crown, cape, etc. Merlin wears tunic and cone hat with stars and quarter moons on them. Sir Elroy wears a loose tunic over tights and carries a "sword." Rebel wears loose garment with black and white stripes and carries a ball and chain (may be Styrofoam). Guards wear identical baggy tunics, tights, and helmets; they carry cardboard spears. Sleeping Beauty wears a long gown slit to reveal shorts and boots. She also wears cape, and cone-shaped hat with scarf. Elroy wears armor in Scene 2.
Properties: Cauldron (may be cardboard) with tall crown inside; slip of paper; signs reading, THE KING IS A

SHORTY, THE KING IS A SHRIMP, THE
KING IS A MIDGET, THE KING IS A
RUNT, and THE NEW KING IS A BEAN-
POLE.
Setting: Scene 1, throne room, with
Gothic windows, coat of arms, etc.,
on walls. There is a large throne cen-
ter with a tasseled cord near throne.
Scene 2, forest, with cardboard
bushes and trees. At left is cave en-
trance, which may be made of black
paper or crepe paper strands near
exit. There is a sign at entrance read-
ing, QUIET ZONE, SLEEPING BEAUTY,
AT REST, DO YE NOT DISTURB.
Lighting: No special effects.

HANSEL, GRETEL, AND CO., INC.

Characters: 2 male; 4 female; 1 male or
female for Narrator.
Playing Time: 15 minutes.
Costumes: Appropriate fairy tale dress.
Godmother carries a wand. Narrator
wears everyday dress.
Properties: Old-fashioned, homemade
brooms (shredded paper on sticks),
sack containing napkins, sack containing string, loaf of bread, bush
with strawberries, "deed."
Setting: Scene 1: Hansel and Gretel's
cottage. Wooden table and chairs are
at center, with fireplace and cupboard
in background. Scenes 2 and 3: the
forest. No set is needed, except a
background of trees, if desired. In
Scene 3, a candy house with gingerbread shingles, peppermint windows,
etc., is added.
Lighting: No special effects.

SNOW WHITE AND FRIENDS

Characters: 3 male; 2 female; 2 male or
female for Mirror and Narrator.
Playing Time: 20 minutes.
Costumes: Appropriate fairy tale costumes. Narrator wears everyday
modern dress. Mirror may wear
sandwich boards. Woodsman carries
an ax.
Properties: Ax, banana, apple.
Setting: Scenes 1 and 3: the Queen's
throne room. A throne is at center.
Scenes 2 and 4: the forest. A stump
is down center.
Lighting: No special effects.

ALADDIN STRIKES IT RICH

Characters: 1 male; 2 female; 3 male or
female for Magic Lamp, Hassan, and
Narrator.
Playing Time: About 15 minutes.
Costumes: Aladdin is barefoot, wears
pants and shirt of tan or light color,
with rope belt. Mother wears plain,
ragged dress and sandals. Hassan has
long robe, turban with jewel in front,
and sandals. Magic Lamp wears
black jacket with string of scarves
stuffed up sleeve or in pocket, carries
wand and paper towels. Jeanie wears
leotard and glittery tights. Narrator
wears modern, everyday dress.
Properties: Box of lamps (lanterns,
flashlights, other various lights and
lamps can be used), paper towels,
scarves, wand (stick covered with
shiny paper), business card for
Hassan.
Setting: Scene 1: Kitchen in Aladdin's
house. Stone walls, window with torn
curtains, bare cupboard, tables and
chairs, fireplace with kettle. Scene 2:
Cave. Dark walls, cobwebs, old boxes
and crates scattered about (one must
be large enough to hold Jeanie, and
one contains lamps), vases and jars
on shelves.
Lighting: No special effects.

SHERWOOD FOREST REVISITED

Characters: 3 male; 1 female; 1 male or

female for Narrator; as many male or female extras as desired for Merry Men (non-speaking parts).

Playing Time: 15 minutes.

Costumes: Robin wears green and has sword. Merry Men are dressed similarly. King and Marian wear appropriate fairy tale costumes. Sheriff wears black eye patch, cowboy hat, and other Western accessories as desired.

Properties: Bag of money.

Setting: Scene 1: King's throne room, with throne, bell rope, and appropriate decorations as desired. Scene 2: Sherwood Forest, with backdrop of trees, if desired.

Lighting: No special effects.

THE SORCERER'S APPRENTICE FINDS A HELPING HAND

Characters: 3 male; 3 female; 2 male or female for Narrator and Hand (non-speaking part).

Playing Time: 20 minutes.

Costumes: Sorcerer wears long black robe with stars and half moons and a pointed hat. He has a long, gray beard. Witch wears black and has pointed hat. Good Fairy wears flowing white dress, jeweled crown. Wife wears plain long robe. Paperboy and Salesman wear leotards and tunics. Wife wears gray wig and veil. She and Sorcerer wear jeans under robes.

Properties: Wands, tongue depressor, "magic dust" (powdered tempera), briefcase containing wand and bottles, wet umbrella, plastic or paper fish, dollar bills, large book, broom.

Setting: The Sorcerer's lab with table holding vials and beakers with tubes running from one to another. There is a tall writing desk with a stool, and near it a large box with a hinged top, in which is concealed the actor playing the Hand. Astrological charts on wall, telescope, old clock, etc., may complete furnishings.

Lighting: No special effects.